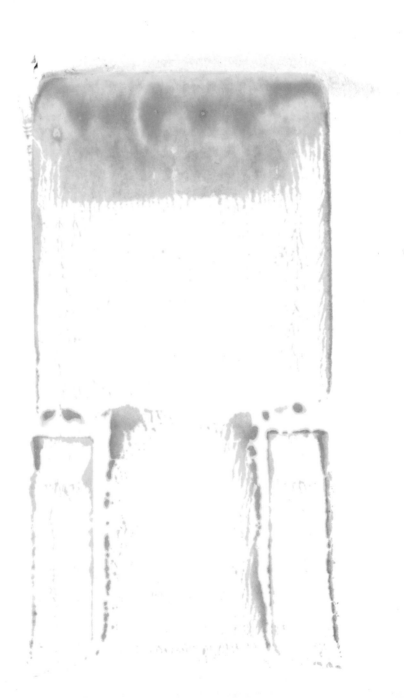

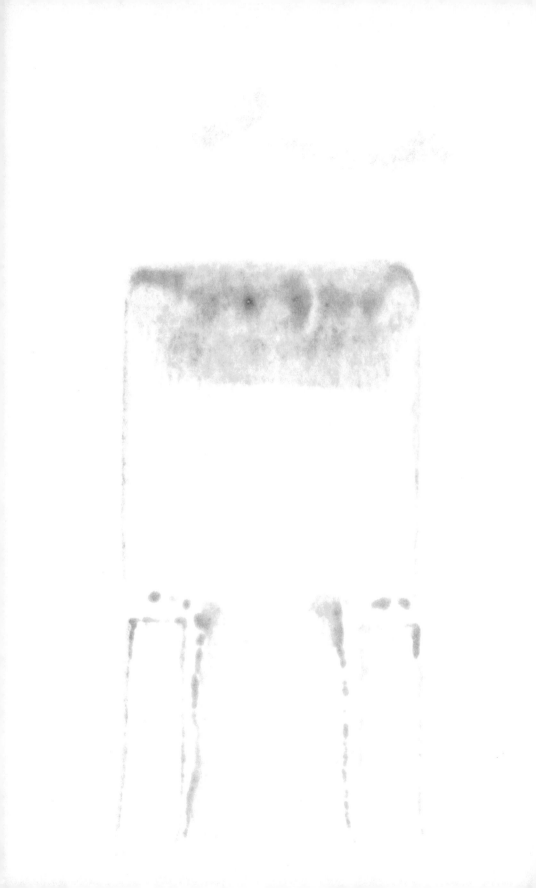

# LIBRARY
# PLANNING
# FOR
# AUTOMATION

*Edited by*
ALLEN KENT

*Director, Knowledge Availability Systems Center*
*University of Pittsburgh*

Based on the proceedings of a conference
held at the University of Pittsburgh, June 2-3, 1964

SPARTAN BOOKS, Inc.     Washington, D. C.
MACMILLAN AND COMPANY, Ltd.     London

# LIBRARY PLANNING FOR AUTOMATION

© 1965 by ALLEN KENT

Printed in the UNITED STATES OF AMERICA

Library of Congress Catalog Card No. 65-17307

Sole Distributors in Great Britain, the British Commonwealth, and the Continent of Europe:

MACMILLAN and COMPANY, Ltd.
10-15 St. Martin's Street
London, W.C. 2

# CONTENTS

# PREFACE

A number of proposals have been made at the executive and legislative levels of the Federal government to alleviate the problems of storage and retrieval of recorded knowledge. One of the recent, far-reaching proposals calls for the development of a National Science Library System.

Dr. Stafford L. Warren, Special Assistant to the President, conceived this system, which would cope with the published periodical literature in science, engineering, social science, and law.

The National Science Library System calls for the establishment of regional centers which would provide a network for the distribution of recorded knowledge on demand.

The regional centers would store, in microfilm, perhaps 30,000-50,000 periodicals in the subject fields covered. These materials would be available to college and university libraries, among others. Computer systems would be developed to permit rapid and precise reaction to user requirements.

What are the implications of this proposal for a National Science Library System, relating to the published periodical literature, for library planning? It is obvious that several factors will be under scrutiny by colleges and universities, including space, equipment, and cost requirements, which would influence library planning. Presumably, collections of greater scope would be available at lesser costs. The question of copyright infringement, however, would be involved to an increasing degree, since much of the periodical literature is distributed by commercial publishers.

In order to scrutinize the Warren proposal, a distin-

guished group of panelists was presented with three
working papers:

1. The Warren proposal.

2. A paper on microform, presenting:
   (a) capital costs for converting the published pe-
       riodical literature to microform;
   (b) costs for stocking colleges and universities with
       microform copies;
   (c) capital equipment costs for storing and view-
       ing the microform;
   (d) costs of preparing full-size copies of materials
       on demand;
   (e) space requirements for necessary equipment.

3. A paper on the influence of automation on the design
   of a university library.

The panels were constituted as follows:

Library planners:
   (a) those having been involved in library construc-
       tion programs recently;
   (b) those now actively planning or in the midst
       of library construction;
   (c) those contemplating library construction with-
       in the next five years.

Periodical publishers:
   (a) commercial publishers;
   (b) nonprofit publishers.

The panelists were asked to react to the Warren proposal and to the other two working papers. These papers as well as the ensuing presentations and discussions are given in the following.

The support of the Council on Library Resources in providing a grant for travel expenses of panelists is gratefully acknowledged.

ALLEN KENT

*Mount Lebanon, Pennsylvania*
January 31, 1965

## CONFERENCE PARTICIPANTS

KENNETH S. ALLEN
*Associate Director*
*University of Washington Libraries*
*Seattle, Washington*

JOHN H. BERTHEL
*Librarian*
*Johns Hopkins University*
*Baltimore, Maryland*

C. RAY CARPENTER
*Executive Director*
*The Survey Committee*
*Milton S. Hershey Medical Center*
*Pennsylvania State University*
*University Park, Pennsylvania*

SAMUEL B. FREEMAN
*President, Micro Photo Division*
*Bell & Howell Company*
*1700 Shaw Avenue*
*Cleveland, Ohio*

GUSTAVE A. HARPER
*Director*
*Boston University Libraries*
*Boston, Massachusetts*

EDWARD M. HEILIGER
*Director of Library and Information Retrieval Services*
*Florida Atlantic University*
*Boca Raton, Florida*

ELMER HUTCHISSON
*Director*
*American Institute of Physics*
*New York, New York*

ALLEN KENT (Conference Chairman)
*Director*
*Knowledge Availability Systems Center*
  *and Professor, Graduate School of Library and Information Sciences*
*University of Pittsburgh*
*Pittsburgh, Pennsylvania*

JOSEPH H. KUNEY
*Director of Business Operations*
*American Chemical Society Applied Publications*
*1155 Sixteenth Street, N. W.*
*Washington, D. C.*

WILLIAM N. LOCKE
*Director of Libraries*
*Massachusetts Institute of Technology*
*Cambridge, Massachusetts*

H. W. MAGOUN
*Dean*
*Graduate Division*
*University of California, Los Angeles*
*Los Angeles, California*

GEORGE G. MALLISON
*Dean*
*School of Graduate Studies*
*Western Michigan University*
*Kalamazoo, Michigan*

JOHN MARKUS
*Manager*
*Information Research*
*McGraw-Hill, Inc.*
*330 West 42nd Street*
*New York, New York*

JOHN H. MORIARTY
*Director of Libraries*
*Purdue University*
*Lafayette, Indiana*

ANDREW D. OSBORN
*Professor of Library Science*
*University of Pittsburgh*
*Pittsburgh, Pennsylvania*

FRAZER G. POOLE
*Librarian*
*The University of Illinois Library*
*Chicago Undergraduate Division*
*Navy Pier*
*Chicago, Illinois*

VICTOR A. SCHAEFER
*Director of Libraries*
*University of Notre Dame*
*Notre Dame, Indiana*

HERBERT SWINBURNE
*Nolen-Swinburne and Associates*
*1601 Locust Avenue*
*Philadelphia, Pennsylvania*

STAFFORD L. WARREN
*Special Assistant to the President*
*The White House*
*Washington, D. C.*

PART I

# THE WORKING PAPERS

# CHAPTER I

# A PROPOSED NATIONAL SCIENCE LIBRARY SYSTEM*

## STAFFORD L. WARREN

*Special Assistant to the President*
*The White House*

## INTRODUCTION

The information explosion resulting from the dramatic increase in research activities produces a critical problem which affects indirectly much of our national defense and economic well-being, and directly our nation's educational and research efforts.

The library has been the heart of educational and research institutions from time immemorial, serving the advanced student, scholar and investigator.

At present each educational and research institution attempts to acquire as large a library holding as its financial support can provide. With the possible exception of the Library of Congress, few libraries have been able to amass a comprehensive holding even of the published scientific literature. Many university libraries

---

*This proposal is part of a study designed to stimulate discussion, prepared in the office of the Special Assistant to Combat Mental Retardation, and, therefore, any opinions expressed are those of the author and do not represent necessarily those of the Administration.

have concentrated, therefore, in some field or discipline—i.e., biomedical, engineering, physics, etc.—to meet a local development within their financial resources. Thus few university libraries are truly the heart of great centers of learning, or even great centers of scientific effort.

The most rapidly growing disciplines of today are in the sciences, the physical, biomedical, and behavioral sciences, by virtue of the tremendous support being poured into them by the Federal agencies.

The great increase of research findings is being published in an ever increasing number and volume of scientific journals which is overwhelming the library system and procedures of today.

Such a chaotic situation has developed in the handling of this large volume of published scientific literature that a new administrative concept is required, namely, that of a single National Library of Science System and network which uses the most sophisticated technological tools available to permit both effective control and use of this otherwise overwhelming volume of literature, and which would give every library access to all of the published scientific literature for its users.

This proposal presents a plan for putting a single comprehensive system in operation before the situation deteriorates further, and before splintering of effort leads to irreversible chaos. The proposal would conserve existing facilities and organizations which would contribute computer and other materials to a single coordinated pool and network under a common standard. Extensive discussion and exploration discloses no alternative but to recommend that the system be a national one, operated by the Federal establishment. The Office of Science and Technology would coordinate the standards required to make the system work effectively in accordance with existing regulations.

The proposed plan, encouraged by the President's

Panel on Mental Retardation, is timely for science as a whole as well as being advantageous to those concerned with research in mental retardation. It would elicit the enthusiastic endorsement of most of the scientific community and of Congress. It would represent a new scientific breakthrough, the first to be proposed by the present Administration.

Tentative suggestions for implementing this proposal follow.*

## BACKGROUND

*Chaos, duplication,* and *waste* are the words used more and more frequently by responsible members of our nation's scientific community to describe the problem they face in being unable to refer effectively to the record of previous research accomplishments.

On the one hand, predominantly Federal expenditures, to support research and development programs, have risen dramatically over the years to the present $15 billion for 1961–62 (almost three times the 1953–54 national level of $5.2 billion). On the other hand, one of the primary means for assuring effective prosecution of research and development programs—convenient access to the scientific literature—has been progressively paralyzed by an archaic library system.

The number of scientists and engineers affected is approximately 1,400,000 with even conservative estimators predicting a doubling in this number in ten years. It has been estimated by some that the professional research specialists spend almost 25 percent of their time seeking useful information from the published literature.

The number of published scientific and technical

---

*This report was approved by the Advisory Committee to the Special Assistant to the President for Mental Retardation with the recommendation that he use every method available to him to implement it as soon as possible.

periodicals, reporting potentially useful results of research, has been estimated at more than 50,000 which contain upward of 1,000,000 articles. (They have been increasing about 10–15 percent each year.)

Evidence of the paralysis of the library system which has attempted traditionally to cope with this problem is not quantitative. However, it has been observed that:

1. Existing and newly created research and university libraries have been able to acquire only a small portion of the published literature, restricting their acquisitions to materials only in the apparent core of the interests of their clientele. Attempts to augment these collections are inhibited by inadequate space for storage and inadequate funds to acquire materials in uncovered areas.

2. Introduction of modern computer technology has been desultory, primarily because few if any libraries have sufficient resources to attempt effective application, and such systems must be worked out cooperatively and on a large scale in order to be successful.

3. Abstracting and indexing services, individually and as a whole, have not produced an integrated solution to the problems of exploiting the published literature, especially one which permits decentralized use in libraries.

4. Research and development on this problem has been supported for a number of years, but results have been fragmentary and have not fit together into an integrated solution.

5. Individual scientists desiring service from libraries are generally unable to conduct efficient literature searches, and even when identifying potentially useful material, often cannot lay hands quickly on the source materials they wish to read.

That this situation exists is well known to most Federal agencies and the nation's librarians. However, only the National Library of Medicine has attacked the problem aggressively with regard to the published periodical literature in designing a computer-based system to permit more effective exploitation of the biomedical publications. However, even this agency has not yet been able to provide service in the depth and breadth that would show signs of alleviating the larger problems.

The problem is also well known to organizations in the private sector, as evidenced by almost every major professional association engaging in the first steps which are aimed at standardizing nomenclature in an effort to work toward computer-based systems. However, these activities have been largely uncoordinated and appear to be chaotic when viewed nationally.

In addition, there has been a proliferation of specialized information centers throughout the nation, variously estimated as 450 to 3,000 in number, which up to now have had no way of coordination into an effective national resource.

Accordingly, a new administrative concept of a National Library of Science System and network is proposed which would build on existing efforts, particularly on the effective start made by the National Library of Medicine.

The new system would not replace any existing libraries, but would greatly improve their capacity to serve their customers and users.

It would reduce the need for stock storage space in every science library.

## PROPOSAL

It is proposed that a National Library of Science System and network be established. It would provide a pool of all the published scientific literature, and the network would make the literature available to all who may wish to use it. Thus any investigator, whether he be in a university, a Federal agency, or in private enterprise, would have access through his nearest library to all of the published scientific literature.

For simplicity at this stage of knowledge, it is recommended that the content of the National Library of Science System be restricted to the open published scientific literature—the scientific journals.

It is recognized that this limitation to the published scientific literature does not satisfy the very important demands and needs of the users of a large segment of the research and development report literature, nor that of the classified literature.

However, the published scientific journals do provide a clearly defined starting point which is stable and where experimentation and experience in the development of standards and procedures can be carried out. If common standards and procedures are applied, there is no reason why the utilization of the system and its network cannot be developed eventually for the appropriate distribution in any desired form of all three types of documents—i.e., the open published literature, the report literature, and the classified literature.

The following steps would be taken to consolidate fragmented activities in coping with the published scientific periodical literature into a single national library pool, or system and network, employing modern computer and related technology; and to facilitate the acquisition, analysis, storage, distribution and searching of these materials:

1. Identify holdings and acquisition programs of the major Federal libraries and professional associations, and by agreement assign to each Federal

library, or other participant, a portion of the list of published scientific publications which each would contribute to the pool or system in the form of tapes or other microform, produced under acceptable standards.

2. Foster agreement between the Federal and private sectors on standards and/or compatible procedures for the acquisition, analysis and coding of scientific articles in the various disciplines.

3. Work toward the ultimate goal of a complete storehouse on tapes of published periodical literature (summaries, abstracts, and citations) which would be fed continuously by existing programs in the Federal and private sectors, and augmented in areas not covered adequately. This storehouse would be available to stock a network of regional centers and other units with tape and eventually microfilm copies of all or selected parts of the scientific literature. The regional centers and other units would serve as distribution points and to stock inexpensively the libraries of organizations throughout the nation. Whenever possible, although at a later phase, create similarly a complete storehouse on microfilm of the published scientific literature.

4. Foster development in universities of curricula for the education of librarians and information scientists who would staff the operating units of the National Library of Science System and its cooperating organizations.

5. Foster development of basic research in the library and information sciences, including semantics, linguistics, philosophy, logic, mathematics and statistics bearing on the field.

## AUTONOMOUS COOPERATING LIBRARIES
## AND SPECIALIZED INFORMATION CENTERS

One of the strengths of the present library system of our nation is the existence of major libraries and specialized information centers which have extensive holdings in one or more subjects or disciplines. These activities may be found in the Federal sector (e.g., National Agricultural Library) as well as in the private sector (e.g., Chemical Abstracts Service). However, except for the Library of Congress, none may be said to have a complete holding in the published scientific literature.

In order to bring the strengths of these organizations to bear on the National Library of Science System, as well as increasing the effectiveness of their own autonomous activities, these organizations will participate in the operation of the system. This participation chiefly will involve providing input to the National Library of Science System in agreed-upon specialized areas of strength while being able, at their own option, to draw on the strengths of other cooperating organizations as well as the complete scientific literature through the system.

It is noteworthy that the work of converting the scientific material onto tape needs to be done only once. The tapes can be replicated cheaply and quickly distributed throughout the network. This feature alone is a great saving in making all of the information available to all in the network.

The analogy to this type of relationship may be seen in the radio and television network of our nation in which local programming, while serving special interests of local audiences, may be tapped for nationwide broadcasting when of general interest.

## OPERATION AND MANAGEMENT

Each one of the existing Federal libraries is a sophisticated operating organization with an assignment designated by statute or executive order.

Any one of them would be capable of managing the proposed national system and providing for the housekeeping purposes and needs. The representation of each one of the Federal agencies and the members from the private sectors on the advisory committee on operations of the system assumes that each field or discipline among the sciences will be properly served. While several alternate administrative and management arrangements are conceivable, only three possibilities are mentioned here:

1. The Library of Congress would form a new division to provide for the operation of the system. The Library of Congress is just now considering computerizing its catalogue system. It has large holdings in the sciences, law and the arts. The large preponderance of its activities concerns books rather than the scientific journals. It is submitted that the Library of Congress concentrate as its assignment on computerizing the holdings in the field of law where a great need exists and where its holdings are preeminent, and consider as an ultimate goal the problem presented by the bound literature in books.

   For law holdings the same distribution system and similar procedures and standards would be employed as in the scientific literature, except that the principal users would be the Congress and other legislative bodies, the courts, the law schools and lawyers.

   Under present circumstances, even with a vigorous program, it would take several years to start to develop such a program. It is recommended that

the Library of Congress undertake the computerization of its holdings in the law.

2.  Create a new agency or commission. While there
    are some advantages to an entirely new organiza-
    tion, it would have to start from the beginning in
    establishing its program, facilities, cooperative at-
    titudes and other arrangements necessary to
    success.

3.  Change and enlarge a going program in an existing
    agency. Each one is beginning to employ computer
    techniques for cataloguing and library purposes
    and plans to enlarge its scope.

    (a)  There are information agencies or services of
         considerable sophistication in each of the de-
         fense agencies. They have restricted or spe-
         cialized fields and purposes, however, which
         might not yield a comfortable environment for
         a broad scale science library system giving li-
         brary service to all users.

    (b)  The Department of Commerce, under P.L. 776
         (81st Congress, 1950), is just now preparing
         plans for the development of the concept of a
         clearing house of Federal scientific and tech-
         nical information from the government's
         activities in the physical and engineering
         sciences. This is a large, difficult, and com-
         plex program not yet crystallized. This area,
         called elsewhere "Government Reports" or
         the "Report Literature," needs special consid-
         eration and does not lend itself readily to the
         National Library of Science System proposed
         here. For the published scientific literature,
         the compatibility of the government report lit-
         erature and the published scientific literature
         are important to each other and each serves

a specific service. It is submitted that the two programs be developed separately, yet use language which can be coordinated.

(c) The National Agricultural Library has large holdings in technical agriculture and has developed a bibliographic network with the land-grant institutions. It has a committee studying the possibilities of automation, but as yet has no formal plan to do so.

(d) The National Library of Medicine has developed in MEDLARS a computerized citation service for *Index Medicus* (titles and authors) in the biomedical published literature. It is admittedly experimental and has defects which become apparent upon trial. The computer and microform techniques lend themselves readily to experimentation and change.

After considerable discussion and reflection, it is recommended that MEDLARS be adopted as the physical and administrative starting point for the National Library of Science System and that it be designated as the Washington Center (or Region I) of the network of seven centers, all having the same total holdings of tapes and microfilm, and each in turn interconnected with local library service centers and other subdivisions which would develop in accordance with practical operational requirements to serve the users.

Leaving the administration under the United States Public Health Service would capitalize upon an existing and staffed computer-based system and relationships already established throughout the nation and foreign countries, and the pooling of the other existing resources within it would permit the National Library of Science

System to become operational at an earlier date, and more economically.

Retention of the existing libraries would permit the extensive and specialized relationships which they have with a broad segment of the scientific sector throughout the country to continue undisturbed and enhanced by the resources of the pool which would be available to them also.

The appointment of the Advisory Committee on Operations could be carried out promptly, and planning could be advanced at a rapid rate.

The National Library of Medicine would become an in-house research unit of the system and continue to carry on its present assignments, except for the operation of the new system.

## ADVISORY COMMITTEE ON OPERATIONS

The Committee will advise the Director on operating policies of the National Library of Science System. It will provide recommendations relating to both input and output functions as well as to the operation of the total system. It will interpret recommendations of the Office of Science and Technology on quality standards and other matters in terms of the needs and interests of the scientific community.

The Committee will consist of 15 members drawn from the Federal and private sectors who represent major scientific disciplines and government agencies engaged in major operating and supporting programs in these disciplines—i.e., the National Agricultural Library, the Library of Congress, the National Library of Medicine, the Department of Commerce, the Department of Defense, the Department of Interior, the Office of Education, the National Science Foundation, and seven at large from the private sector.

The members of the Committee will be appointed by the President to four-year terms, with option for reappointment, upon recommendation of the Director, with the advice of the various professional societies and appropriate government agencies.

## ADVISORY COUNCILS AND STUDY SECTIONS

In order to develop the extramural program, it is recommended that an advisory council and study section system advisory to the Director be appointed after the pattern so successful in developing the program of the National Institutes of Health.

The vigorous and rapid development of education and training programs, research and development, design and construction of the facilities and hardware and the organization of conferences on standards and other aspects of the program are required. Both the participation and the advice of knowledgeable professionals in the private sector would be incorporated in the planning and development of the program in these advisory groups.

## USERS OF THE NATIONAL LIBRARY OF SCIENCE SYSTEM

The new system will serve several levels of users, ranging from the institution at one end of the spectrum to the individual scientist or student at the other.

The institution, for example, a university or an industrial research organization, will be served by having its library stocked on a custom basis with replicas, in microform, of the published scientific literature; and, if desired, with replicas, in searchable form, of the results of analysis performed by the processing agencies which feed the system. Thus, this library will be able to provide decentralized service to its clientele, but backed up by the total input of the system. Thus, every library which wishes to do so, may have access to the total holdings of the system at any time, and to serve its users in any one of the disciplines served by the published scientific literature or journals.

The individual will be served by being able to obtain, on demand, facsimiles of published articles or their abstracts or summaries. Also, he will be able to have custom searches performed based on specific inquiries, with results of searches provided in the form of bibliographic citations, abstracts or summaries, and/or facsimiles of the full texts of articles.

## WASHINGTON OPERATIONS HEADQUARTERS— REGION I

The Washington headquarters of the National Library of Science System would consist of a number of components:

1. The Headquarters cadre for the system.
2. The Washington regional center of the system— Region I.
3. The National Libraries of Medicine, Agriculture, Congress, Commerce, Department of Defense, Interior and Federal cooperating libraries which would serve the in-house research and development program for the system.

Elements 2 and 3 are discussed elsewhere in this plan. Element 1, the Headquarters cadre, would include the Director and his Deputies; an operational staff to perform housekeeping operations; and a staff to assist the Advisory Committee on Operations and the Advisory Council and Study Sections.

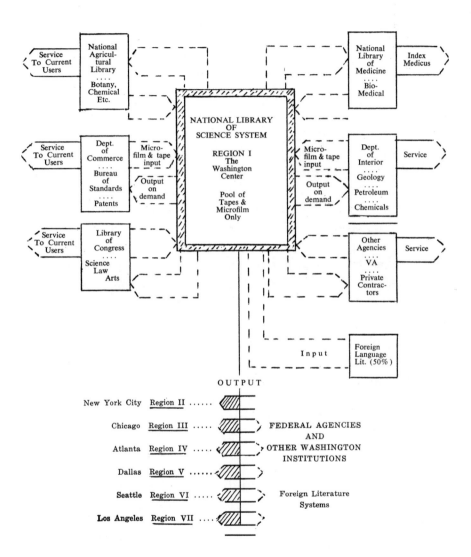

Figure 1.—*Information Flow—Input and Output Examples of Operation of Regional Center.*
Prepared by
    Office of the Special Assistant to the President for Mental Retardation, 2/10/64,

## THE COMPATIBILITY OF SYSTEMS—
## THE NEED FOR ONE STANDARD

At the present time there are many computer systems with their own program and code arrangements for filing and retrieving information. They are usually incompatible because they cannot "talk" with each other. This is both frustrating and costly.

It is recognized that present computer systems are experimental and that both experience and new developments may bring about great changes as the operation of these systems continues.

In this chaotic situation, the dilemma could be met by proceeding with one of the existing systems until the recommendations can be made by the Office of Science and Technology for a uniform national standard which can be used throughout the National Library of Science System. The Bureau of Standards, among others, is now actively working on this problem of standards.

It is fortunate that the computer is such a flexible tool for the conversion from one system to another is possible. However, so much is at stake in doing so that it becomes urgent that standards be met at an early date so the changes hopefully need only be done once and early in the development of this new system.

## STANDARDS

There are two types of standards that will be fostered by the National Library of Science System.

The first type relates to the standard format required for the physical manipulation of inputs and outputs of the system. The other type relates to the standards, or sets of compatible standards, which are useful for the intellectual manipulation of inputs and outputs.

The first type is amenable to engineering evaluation. The second type, which is not, will be approached experimentally with procedures used and subject, for a considerable period, to constant examination and revision.

It is likely that considerable experimentation will be required for at least a decade before the systems and standards reach a steady state.

## REGIONAL CENTERS

Several classes of regional centers, distribution units and service units are planned. In addition, there will be an additional element in the National Library of Science System consisting of autonomous cooperating libraries and specialized information centers. All centers, regardless of class, will be equipped with suitable computers and related equipment to permit them to serve functions of input and output for the system. The cooperating elements will be equipped to conduct specialized input and output functions related to their autonomous activities. The computer technique lends itself readily to the size of the need and use in any particular situation.

*Input functions* will consist of acquisition of periodicals, analysis of articles, coding, storage of coded information in machine-readable form, storage of source materials in microform, and transmission of replicas of coded information and of source materials in microform to other units in the system. As a result of the ease of replication and distribution of input materials, the input of any item needs to occur only once in any part of the system.

*Output functions* will consist of bulk or selective dissemination of processed materials to organizations engaging in decentralized exploitation functions, and response to custom questions.

Each of the centers and autonomous cooperating libraries and specialized information centers, in addition to input and output functions, will participate in activities relating to preparation of glossaries, codes, and standards, and wherever possible in research and educational and inservice training programs of the university, thus reducing the need for duplication of training resources elsewhere.

Fortunately, there already exists a communication network (telephone, telegram, military, National Communication System), the use of which makes possible inexpensive, prompt, and continuous exchange of information on electromagnetic tapes among any number of centers so that the pool can be continuously filled wherever it is desired to do so.

## SITES OF REGIONAL CENTERS

The selection of sites for establishing centers will be based on various factors. A primary criterion for selection will be proximity to loci of scientific competence and demonstrated competence in the information science.

It is proposed that primary centers replicating the total pool be given consideration of being established on Veterans Administration land, particularly because of the strong relationships of the VA with, and proximity to, the scientific community in general, and universities in particular.

The smaller secondary and tertiary centers will hold a less extensive part of the pool or a suecialized part. In order to take advantage of existing information processing activities in the private sector, the smaller centers will be established at sites in close proximity to the strongest of these, i.e., in relationship to the density of users.

## OPERATION OF CENTERS AND
## UNITS BY PRIVATE CONTRACT

There is extensive testimony in the literature and Congressional hearings of the inextricable relationship of education, research and inservice training in many scientific fields, and particularly in medicine. The past experience of the Federal government with university management of contractual programs has been excellent.

It is recommended that the National Library of Science System explore contractual arrangements with universities having educational and research programs in the library sciences for undertaking a service responsibility for a unit of any predetermined size combined with education and research in the library sciences and allied fields.

Such an arrangement would permit great flexibility in the training of the special manpower needed in this and similar programs, would promote research efforts and focus the service in an area having a high concentration of users.

There should be a close working relationship with the Dean's Committees of the VA facilities and their respective universities in this connection.

## MANPOWER FOR THE SYSTEM

Specialized professional manpower in the library and information sciences will be required in considerable quantity to staff the National Library of Science System.

Professionals in this field are in very short supply, and only a few universities have yet established curricula which can provide competent specialists in sufficient numbers.

Accordingly, one of the first priorities of the system will be to foster the development of curricula throughout the nation, and with the advice of its Advisory Council, arrange for fellowships in sufficient number to attract the necessary individuals into the program.

The need for research support and the interrelationship between advanced education and research, and

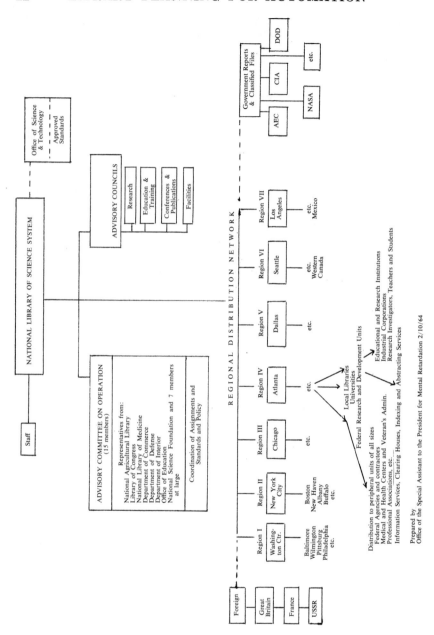

Figure 2.

Prepared by
Office of the Special Assistant to the President for Mental Retardation,
2/10/64.

equipment and facilities, in support of the education of the advanced student must be coordinated and supported in these considerations.

## ROLE OF THE SCIENTIFIC JOURNALS

Accountability with regard to expenditure of our nation's resources for scientific research and development cannot be managed by preparation of financial balance sheets. Rather, the balance sheets are maintained in the scientific publication or journal where accountability is measured in terms of full disclosure of experimental work performed, to peers in similar and dissimilar disciplines, so that the adjudicative procedure in the search for truth may proceed step by step, democratically and soundly, in full public view with access to the record assured to all who desire to read it.

The ultimate goal of the National Library of Science System is to record all of the scientific publications in tape and film within the pool and make them available in all or part to any legitimate user. The National Library of Science System will plan to take advantage of this resource in several respects. Cooperation from the journal editors, their advisory boards and the professional societies which sponsor them will be fostered in:

1. Developing glossaries covering the disciplinary interests of each journal.
2. Participating in the analysis activities (e.g., abstracting, indexing, coding).
3. Participating in other processing activities (e.g., microfilming of articles) as local facilities may permit.

It is probable eventually that each author will desire to or be required to furnish his own abstract and summary acceptable to the editor of the journal and the National Library of Science System.

Many professional associations have appointed committees to work on the problems envisaged here and some have already prepared glossaries, abstracting services, etc., which can be coordinated and integrated within the system when the basic codes and standards are adjusted to make it possible to do so.

There is a great and unmet need for a more rapid exchange of information than by journal publication, particularly within the defense industries, and rather more concerning engineering research and development than in basic sciences.

Obviously much word of mouth or letter exchanges of information occur among small groups. There is a tendency to keep the information informal until it is disclosed in a review or symposium rather than as a published scientific article. Some go so far as to predict that authorities in a field will announce their conclusions in some fashion, perhaps putting them directly on tapes and into the kind of system proposed here without their ever appearing in the usual published scientific open literature.

If the journals disappear as a means of dissemination of information, to be replaced by other methods, there still remains the need to have a repository of some sort in which the information is filed, stored and retrieved. For the foreseeable future, the computerized system proposed here is a convenient library tool of great promise displacing nothing but the need for great library stacks and adding great flexibility and depth to the ordinary scientific service library.

## LIBRARY UTILIZATION OF JOURNALS

It is recommended that libraries and individuals continue to subscribe to scientific journals and to keep them available for the usual use for about five years.

Even though this same material would be available in the National Library of Science System pool, great advantages accrue to the scholar and the student by browsing among the journals in the stacks and library shelves. Browsing in such an environment provides a serendipity which plays a great role in the development of research and of the mind of the student. The computer pool cannot fulfill this important function.

## GOVERNMENT REPORTS

The problem of handling the large volume of government reports has been extensively considered in excellent reports by the President's Scientific Advisory Committee as well as by many agencies. From time to time government reports result in publication in the scientific literature in which case they would in due course come into the pool of the National Library of Science System through established channels.

However, it would be a great convenience to the agencies and the consultants and investigators if the same glossaries and codes were employed so that a similar search program could be available within the National Library of Science System pool and that of the government reports.

The Office of Science and Technology and the Department of Commerce and the appropriate agencies might confer on the usefulness of uniformity and compatibility in the two programs. As stated elsewhere, the computer technology has a great inherent flexibility so that subsequent adjustments for compatibility can be made with comparatively little difficulty. Thus the development and operation of a system does not need to be halted while debate on standards and codes is underway.

## CLASSIFIED LITERATURE

Classified literature is the responsibility of the defense agencies.

A great deal of progress has been made in developing glossaries and standards and computerized techniques in the development of library programs for the classified files in the defense agencies, and particularly by the Defense Document Center.

If the same system of standards, codes and procedures were to be applied in the classified literature, the government report and the published scientific literature, a great convenience would obviously accrue to all concerned.

The role of the Office of Science and Technology and the Federal Council for Science and Technology in coordinating these standards is clear. The presence of a representative of the Department of Defense as a member of the Advisory Committee on Operations of the National Library of Science System would assist in the appropriate integration of the systems, even though they were kept separate in operation.

Only properly cleared persons would have access to appropriate portions of the classified files. Ideally, upon full development and integration of all three systems, a properly cleared person could simultaneously search the open scientific literature, the government report literature and the classified literature.

## THE LEGAL LITERATURE—
## THE LIBRARY OF CONGRESS

Earlier mention of the difficulty in defining limitations to the disciplines in defining the scientific literature applies to the publications of the legal profession and others as well.

There is considerable and important overlap in many fields and already obvious, e.g., medico-legal, patents, engineering, etc. Many efforts are being made by committees in the law schools, the American Bar Foundation, etc., to utilize modern computers and other techniques as library tools in this field.

The Library of Congress has one of the great law libraries of the world. It is recommended that these new techniques be utilized by the Library of Congress to provide tapes and microfilm of the journals and other aspects of the legal literature prepared under the same standards used elsewhere in the National Library of Science System and coordinated through its membership on the advisory committee for operations of the National Library of Science System. By becoming a specialized part of the comprehensive system, it can utilize the same input-output distribution system available to the National Library of Science System. It could serve law libraries and schools, courts and other users as requested.

Coordination of its other holdings would be negotiated through the advisory committee for operations of the National Library of Science System whenever it is appropriate to do so.

## THE OTHER LITERATURE

For this stage of development, this proposal is directed to alleviating a most urgent need—that of providing to the investigator a rapid, accurate and comprehensive search of the published scientific literature or journals.

Obviously there is an even greater volume of literature, particularly that in all sorts of published books, which has been left untouched by this proposal. The collection of books and manuscripts for museum purposes is also a different category which obviously does not lend itself to these techniques, except for microfilming. It is recommended that the proposal be restricted to the published scientific journals and legal documents at this stage of the art.

## FOREIGN LITERATURE

About 50 percent of the total scientific literature is published in foreign journals. There has been considerable discussion within the International Council of Scientific Unions about the complex problems of devising suitable and acceptable standards for computer-based library technology and systems in order that a worldwide exchange of information may be possible.

Informal statements by some members on international committees dealing with this subject indicate that any leadership given by the United States would be greatly appreciated and would speed up the arrival of a workable acceptance of standards.

Upon arriving at this state of agreement, the exchange of tapes and microfilm between a National Library of Science System and foreign library sources can be simply done.

It is urgent that research and development of translation machines be expedited for they would be very useful if available.

## COPYRIGHT CONSIDERATIONS

Several mechanisms are available in order to protect publishers from potential losses in income that may eventuate from use of microfilm copies of the periodical literature:

1. Establishing a plan which would involve prepurchase of stamps which would be affixed to copies of articles prepared from microfilm as evidence of royalty payment.

2. Contracting with publishers for preparation of microfilm copies or tapes of their periodicals which would be purchased outright for use in stocking the regional and cooperating centers.

## STANDARDIZATION STEPS

1. Announcement of the program to the scientific community.

   (a) Message by the President to scientists and engineers and to their professional associations, calling for cooperation in the program and in the establishment of standards.

   (b) Request to professional associations to include programs on standards at their national meetings.

2. Action program.

   (a) Set up a national conference on standards with representatives of the professional associations and other organizations responsible for the publishing and processing of the scientific literature.

   (b) Establishment of committees within the professional associations, with paid secretariats, to arrive at standards in the several disciplines within the framework of the advisory council.

   (c) Establishment by the councils of proposed working agreements among the professional associations to rationalize differences among the proposed standards.

   (d) Assignment by the director to the professional associations the responsibility of providing the special codes and glossaries required to file their publications which they sponsor in their journals in the system, after the basic standards have been rationalized and agreed to.

## LEGISLATION REQUIRED

1. To create the National Library of Science System, its regional and peripheral units, the Advisory Committee on Operations and the Advisory Councils and extramural grant program.

2. Approve some administrative organization for the new National Library of Science System which would create a regional unit (The Washington Center) based on the National Library of Medicine and its MEDLARS system, which would be enlarged. The National Library of Science System would be a part of the Department of Health, Education and Welfare, and the organization and functions of the National Library of Medicine would otherwise remain the same.

3. To establish the following functions of the National Library of Science System:

   (a) Design and construction of physical facilities.
   (b) Purchase of capital equipment.
   (c) Foster standards activities in consultation with the Office of Science and Technology.
   (d) Processing and distribution of the periodical literature throughout the system.
   (e) Foster curriculum development in consultation with the Office of Education.
   (f) Foster basic research in consultation with the National Science Foundation and the Department of Health, Education and Welfare.
   (g) Establish policy of using contracts for operation of any parts of the system by universities.
   (h) With the advice of the Office of Science and Technology, foster collaboration, coordination

and integration of the Federal and private libraries and special programs in operation of the input and output of the pool.

## THE BUDGET

There are several parts to consider and the following suggestions are tentative only because they are based on a very preliminary study of the problem.

The budget for the first year, 1964–65, should be for organizing and planning, designing, conferences and pilot programs and education and research programs.

Suggested Budget—Tentative Only (Millions of dollars)

| | 1964–65 | 1965–66 | 1966–67 | Total, 3 years | 1967–68 | 1968–69 | 1969–70 | Total |
|---|---|---|---|---|---|---|---|---|
| Extramural grants Education and training ........ | 2.0 | 4.5 | 5.0 | 11.5 | | | | |
| Research and development (including pilot programs) ...... | 5.0 | 15.0 | 25.0 | 45.0 | | | | |
| Conferences and planning ........ | 2.0 | 2.5 | 1.5 | 6.0 | | | | |
| Facilities Washington, D. C. center planning .. | 1.0 | 1.0 | — | 2.0 | | | | |
| Regional centers and units ....... | — | 3.0 | 50.0 | 53.0 | | | | |
| Operation ....... | — | 1.75 | 3.0 | 4.75 | | | | |
| *Total, first 3 years* . | 10.0 | 27.75 | 84.5 | 122.25 | | | | |
| Extramural grants . | | | | | 31.5 | 35.0 | 40.0 | 106.5 |
| Facilities ......... | | | | | 35.0 | 25.0 | — | 50.0 |
| Operation ........ | | | | | 8.0 | 10.0 | 12.0 | 30.0 |
| *Total, second 3 years* | | | | | 64.5 | 70.0 | 52.0 | 186.5 |

Figure 3.

For the second year, 1965–66, construction could be added for three centers and remodeling and construction and hardware for the beginning of the network of service centers, presumably mostly as pilot programs in large university libraries. The expansion of the centers and service units would continue through 1966–67.

The development should then be reviewed and an appropriate budget proposal for additional activities and continued operation prepared from experience derived up to that point.

## ACKNOWLEDGMENTS

The plan for the National Library of Science System follows recommendations made by the President's Panel on Mental Retardation in its report of October 16, 1962, which cited the problem of scientific communication as being one of serious concern. Similar concern has been expressed by the Advisory Committee to the Special Assistant to the President for Mental Retardation. The conception of the plan for the system has benefited from the work of the President's Science Advisory Committee and many other reports of Federal and private groups and individuals.

Informal discussions during the past year on the need for some solution to the problem and its relationships have been held with representatives to many organizations in the Federal and private sectors, including:

Bureau of the Budget
Department of Commerce
National Science Foundation
Department of Health, Education and Welfare, including:

Public Health Service,
Office of Education, and
National Library of Medicine

American Documentation
    Institute
Council on Library Resources
Federation of American
    Societies for Experimental
    Biology
Veterans Administration
Office of Science and
    Technology

Brown University
Colorado State University
University of Alaska
University of California at Los Angeles
University of Pittsburgh
University of Missouri
University of Washington
and many University committees and librarians
and knowledgeable individuals.

Thus, the proposal has been synthesized from the ideas and suggestions of many. Since it has had many changes during the course of discussion, few may recognize their suggestions in this final plan. However, I have appreciated their dedication and unselfish participation without stint. Our reward will be sufficient if this proposal results in some kind of definitive action to solve this great and important problem—that of making a comprehensive library service available to all who wish to use it.

# CHAPTER 2

# MICROPHOTOGRAPHY OF SOURCE DOCUMENTS FOR THE PROPOSED NATIONAL SCIENCE LIBRARY SYSTEM

SAMUEL B. FREEDMAN

*Former President, Micro Photo Division*
*Bell & Howell Company*
*Cleveland, Ohio*

## INTRODUCTION

In his report, *A Proposed National Science Library System*, Dr. Stafford Warren has introduced an interesting and exciting concept. This system would provide a pool of published scientific literature available to all who may wish to use it. The proposal assigns a role to the microforms as a medium for the storage and acquisition of scientific journals.

Our assignment is to react to the Warren proposal for a National Science Library System, particularly with regard to the use of microforms for storage and delivery of information.

Therefore, in this report I will attempt to outline the feasibility of the use of microforms in the National Science Library System. We will review very briefly some of the history of the microforms, describe some of the microforms presently available and their uses, and examine the possibility of their use in the system.

In the process, more questions may be raised than will be answered, but it is important to uncover these now in the discussion stage.

## BRIEF BACKGROUND OF THE MICROFORMS

In the National Microfilm Association's publication, *Glossary of Terms*, a microimage is described as "A unit of information, such as a page of text or a drawing, too small to be read by the unaided eye."

While history tells us that the first microphotograph was produced by Dancer in 1839, it was not until the 1920s that modern microfilming began to make a place for itself commercially. The first major application was in bank record keeping and this remains to this day a very important microfilming function. Other early applications for microfilm were principally related to record protection and space conservation.

The 1930s saw the real beginning of the use of the microform in the publications field. A few progressive newspapers began programs for the microfilming of their issues and there was a beginning in the microfilming of some periodical literature for use in libraries.

The coming of World War II provided a tremendous stimulus to the use of the microimage through the many programs for the preservation of technical files, such as engineering drawings, and for the protection of archival material in danger of destruction through bombing. The V-Mail Program was very effective and demonstrated the possibilities of microfilm as a medium for compressing information, transporting it into another area, and reproducing it in hard-copy form.

The years after World War II through the present time have seen a steady increase in the use of the microimage, and there have been a number of significant developments which contributed to this steady growth.

Possibly the most important development in this period was the development of printout equipment. One type was the reader-printer which permitted the user of a microimage to view the image on a reader screen and then to retrieve a paper copy within seconds, if required, on the same machine.

The other printout development was the Xerox Copyflo which produces hard copy rapidly from roll film or aperture-mounted microfilm on a continuous, high-production basis.

Roll film (Fig. 1), which has the ability to solve

Figure 1.—Roll microfilm.

many problems, was found to be inflexible for some applications. This fact led to the development of a number of cut-film formats, such as:

The aperture card (Fig. 2) was developed during World War II by John Langan and his associates who were working in the OSS. They took a machine tabulating card, cut an aperture in the card, and mounted a frame of microfilm in the aperture.

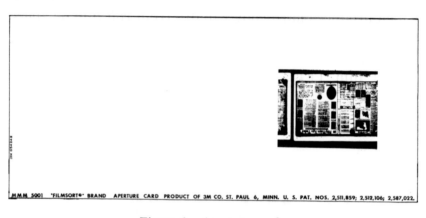

MMM 5001   "FILMSORT" BRAND   APERTURE CARD   PRODUCT OF 3M CO. ST. PAUL 6, MINN. U. S. PAT. NOS. 2,511,859; 2,512,106; 2,587,022.

Figure 2.—Aperture card.

The aperture card found acceptance in the engineering drawing area and in the storage of other information, because revised and additional data could now be slipped into the proper place in the file while the obsolete card could be removed. This flexibility was not practical with roll film. By punching information into the card containing the film frame, it was now possible to select and retrieve information through the use of tabulating machines.

Film jacket (Fig. 3) made it possible to unitize groups of microimages—the roll film was cut into strips and inserted into the sleeves of the jacket. An eye-readable title was placed at the top of the jacket describing the contents. Some applications of the film jacket are

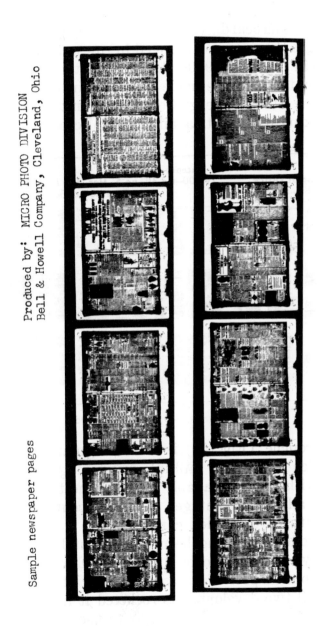

Produced by: MICRO PHOTO DIVISION
Bell & Howell Company, Cleveland, Ohio

Sample newspaper pages

Figure 3.—Film jacket.

found in reports, newspaper clipping files, hospital case history records, and others.

The Microcard (Fig. 4), an opaque card with photographic images arranged in rows, came into serious usage in the early 1950s. Periodical literature and scholarly materials were made available in this format. In 1952 the Atomic Energy Commission initiated a program of making its reports available on Microcard.

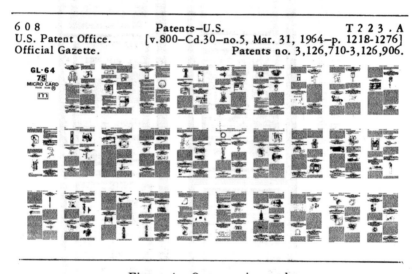

Figure 4.—Opaque microcard.

Microfiche (Fig. 5), is a rectangular sheet of film on which are placed multiple microimages arranged in rows with an eye-readable index at the top of the card. It has all the advantages of translucent film plus the flexibility of the index card concept.

Microfiche has long been known but little used until recently. It began to be utilized in Europe during the 1930s, but its potential was not appreciated in this country until two developments rocketed it into prominence. One was the decision of NASA to use microfiche in its report distribution program. The other was the success of the Thomas Micro-Catalog System.

NILES WEEKLY REGISTER. Baltimore, Maryland  MP
Vol. 72  Pages.  321-384

Figure 5—Microfiche.

Another approach to the solution of the problem of the inflexibility of the roll film was in the electronic selection of images through coding in roll or cut-film format. The integrated film systems combine the photographic images with the coding, both being on the same film. A start in this direction was made in the 1920's, and the first Bush Rapid Selector was constructed during the period 1938 through 1940. There are a number of sophisticated integrated systems on the market today.

## EXAMINATION OF VARIOUS MICROFORMS AS THE STORAGE MEDIUM FOR THE NATIONAL SCIENCE LIBRARY SYSTEM

For purposes of discussion it is necessary to examine various alternative methods available in relation to the requirements as outlined in Dr. Warren's proposal. We believe the requirements to be essentially as follows:

1. High compression storage capability.
2. Low cost and rapid reproduction capabilities film-to-film.
3. Film-to-hard-copy reproduction capability.
4. Format compatible with moderately priced reading equipment.
5. High image quality.
6. Economical input capability.
7. Format compatible with a computer-based search system.

We will now examine microforms in relation to the stated requirements.

### Aperture Cards

The aperture card was not designed primarily to contain multiple images. It was designed to contain one frame of microfilm, thus giving a maximum amount of flexibility. While there are applications where two or more frames are placed in an aperture card, its limited capacity would not achieve the high compression storage capability required in this system. Further, the cost would be quite high in comparison with other mediums.

### Film Jackets

This form does not lend itself to film-to-film reproduction as required here. Essentially, the jacket performs the same function as the microfiche except that it is more expensive when multiple copies are required, and requires more filing space.

### Opaque Microcard

The Microcard has been a valuable medium and gained a good acceptance because of the demand for a microform offering the flexibility of the vertical card file. However, it has certain disadvantages, among which are difficulty in producing hard copy from the Microcard, and the impracticality of making card-to-card copies. The quality of the projected image from the opaque is not as good as the image from translucent film at comparable reduction ratios.

### Integrated Combination Storage and Retrieval Systems

Dr. Warren's report contemplates a separate computer-based search system. It would, therefore, be of no value to incorporate an expensive search system as a part of the film. The combination systems require expensive hardware not compatible with the requirements stated above.

### Roll Microfilm

While the roll microfilm has many good applications and will continue to be of great value, we do not believe that it is the best medium for this system. One of the requirements here is to be able quickly to reproduce information from the file at the center, and it is easier, we believe, to handle a microfiche on this basis.

Roll film does not lend itself to segment duplication such as would be required in this system. For instance, 60 frames on a roll of film would leave you with a short roll or strip of film which would need a leader and a trailer. Titling and filing of such a strip would be a problem.

A quick search on roll microfilm requires more expensive reading equipment—possibly of the cartridge type.

### Microfiche

If there were no other reasons for adopting microfiche for the National Science Library System, the fact that NASA, AEC, and OTS have adopted this medium would possibly be sufficient. There are valid reasons to make the National Science Library System compatible with the microfiche produced by these agencies.

However, there are sufficient additional points of advantage for microfiche in this application that would indicate that it is the proper medium. We believe microfiche qualifies under all points in the requirements for this system:

1. Microfiche has excellent storage compression capabilities. (See "Housing and Space Requirements.")
2. Microfiche lends itself to quick and economical card-to-card reproduction.
3. Microfiche has film-to-hard-copy reproduction capabilities as needed in the system.
4. The microfiche will more readily than other mediums make possible the development of good, low-cost reading equipment in addition to those now available.
5. Microfiche affords the high image quality of translucent film.
6. Microfiche is a very economical microform (see cost breakdown, Fig. 6).
7. Format is compatible with a computer-based search system.

In recommending the use of microfiche for the National Science Library System, we do not want to create the impression that microfiche is the best medium for all applications. The other mediums described have their places and, properly used, will continue to perform valuable functions.

## MICROFICHE AS THE STORAGE MEDIUM FOR THE NATIONAL SCIENCE LIBRARY SYSTEM

Assuming the use of the microfiche as the storage medium for the journals, we will now examine the practical areas of acquisition, production, standards, costs, and flow of information.

### Acquisition of the Scientific Journals

Once it is decided which titles, current and retrospective, are to be included in this program, the matter of acquisition will have to be solved.

In the case of current periodicals, there should be no problem as far as acquisition of originals is concerned. Sets would normally be available from a number of libraries, or a subscription to the journal would provide the copies necessary for the filming process.

The acquisition of back files can be a more difficult problem, since complete sets are not always available and it would be necessary to secure the cooperation of libraries holding these retrospective titles in order to make copies available for filming.

In the case of both the current issues and the retrospective titles, there is the matter of the interest of publishers holding copyright. Copyright is given consideration in Dr. Warren's report, and it is stated that several mechanisms are available in order to protect publishers.

### Production of Microfiche
### from the Original Journals

There are several alternative methods by which the master and the microfiche copies, which will stock the centers, can be produced.

1. An "In-House" centralized operation could be set up at one point by the National Science Library System. This could include only the camera equipment with the processing of the master film and the copies for the centers being produced in an outside laboratory. The centralized operation could, if it seemed advisable, set up a complete processing laboratory in addition to the filming operation.

2. One or more contractors could be engaged to produce the microfiche master and copies.
3. A decentralized filming program could be worked
   out with a number of participants having responsibility for producing master microfiche and copies
   for the centers.
4. Microfiche could be purchased from the publishers
   who would arrange for the production of the microfiche of their own publications.
5. A combination of any of the methods mentioned
   above.

The best way to arrange for the production of the
microfiche cannot be determined at this time. This is
a subject for study before firm conclusions can be arrived at.

## Standards

Although it would be possible in the case of many
journals to place more than 60 pages on a microfiche,
thus reducing costs somewhat, our analysis will be based
on the 60-page format.

The Atomic Energy Commission, NASA, and the Office of Technical Services are engaged in programs to
make available report literature through distribution of
microfiche. These agencies have adopted the same standard which places 60 pages on a microfiche. It is reported
that the Department of Defense will also adhere to these
standards for its own distribution.

As Dr. Warren points out, the report literature is a
part of the store of scientific information and it would
seem logical that the same standards be adopted for the
National Science Library System.

The salient points of the standards adopted by the government agencies are that an overall size microfiche of
105 X 148 mm (approximately 6 X 4 in.) will be used,

and the format of 60 pages arranged in five horizontal rows of twelve pages each will be the standard (up to 72 pages on trailer cards). Mechanical requirements such as frame size, reduction ratio, titling, etc. are included in the standards. Copies of these standards are available from the government agencies or from the National Microfilm Association.

Uniform standards should permit interchange and interfiling of information. It should permit the production of microfiche by various laboratories, and should encourage the development of more and better equipment.

Assuming a 60-page-per-microfiche format, and a total of 10,000,000 pages of periodicals, it is estimated that the master negative could be produced for $300,000. (This figure does not include such costs as may be involved in acquisition of originals or possible royalty payments.)

The production of the master film is a one-time expenditure and, thereafter, copies can be made at a fraction of the master cost. The estimated cost per complete duplicate copy made from the master negative is $25,000. The cost per-page, per-copy, reduces as more copies are produced and the cost of the master film is spread over a larger number of duplicate prints. The table below illustrates this point:

| No. of copies | Negative cost | Duplicate cost @ $25,000 each | Total cost, neg. & pos. | Cost per copy | Cost per page |
|---|---|---|---|---|---|
| 7 | $300,000 | $ 175,000 | $ 475,000 | $68,000 | .0068 |
| 15 | 300,000 | 375,000 | 675,000 | 45,000 | .0045 |
| 50 | 300,000 | 1,250,000 | 1,550,000 | 31,000 | .0031 |
| 100 | 300,000 | 2,500,000 | 2,800,000 | 28,000 | .0028 |
| 500 | 300,000 | 12,500,000 | 12,800,000 | 25,600 | .00256 |
| 1,000 | 300,000 | 25,000,000 | 25,300,000 | 25,300 | .00253 |

From the figures above, it is readily seen that the cost per copy, even at the highest point based on seven copies, is quite modest in relation to the value of the material included.

It is realistic to speculate that 100 libraries throughout the world would be interested in this file at a price of $28,000 for 10,000,000 pages.

Figure 6.—Costs.

Costs

Using a figure of 10,000,000 pages of periodicals, it is estimated that the seven copies for the Regional Centers, including the cost of the master film, could be produced for a total of approximately $475,000, or approximately $68,000 per copy. If one hundred libraries other than the seven centers would purchase the same material, the estimated cost per set would drop to $28,000 per copy.

Not included in these figures are the costs of acquisition, royalties, and other costs incidental to the production of the film.

Housing and Space Requirements

Since Dr. Warren's report indicated the use of a computer-based search system, and the retention of original journals for about five years, consideration in this report is given only to the accession method of filing microfiche. If filing were to be accomplished by title, consideration would have to be given to the expansion space problem.

Microfiche has remarkable ability to compress a large amount of information into a very small space. Based on 10,000,000 pages with 60 pages per microfiche, there would be required approximately 180,000 microfiche of 105 X 148-mm size. Filing is at the rate of approximately 100 cards per inch. Thus, there is a requirement for 1,800 inches of linear filing space or 150 linear feet. The 180,000 microfiche could be filed in four standard 6 X 4-in. filing cabinets in a space 65 in. long, 27 in. deep, and 52 in. high; or an area of approximately 55 cubic feet. The space for the entire filing area, including aisle space, would be approximately 100 cubic feet.

Microfiche can also be housed in standard permanent containers, each holding 100 cards. These boxes can be filed economically on ordinary book shelving. With the thickness of the box included, filing is at the rate of 1¼ in. per 100 film cards. Thus, with these boxes there is a need of 2,250 linear inches, or about 190 linear feet of shelf space.

Using 7-foot-high shelving and figuring two rows of boxes per foot of height, this would mean a space requirement of approximately 15 linear feet of 7-foot-high shelving.

This is a dramatic illustration of compression of information when compared with the space requirements for a periodical file of 10,000,000 pages. We believe the microfiche will occupy less than 3 percent of the shelving space required by the originals.

We have discussed only the space for the microfiche itself. Of course, space will also have to be provided for readers, reader-printers, and for microfiche-to-microfiche duplicating equipment where required. It is not the function of this discussion to comment on the amount of reading and printout equipment that will be required at each library or other point of use. We believe that the librarians will be far better equipped to answer this question.

## FLOW OF INFORMATION THROUGH THE NATIONAL SCIENCE LIBRARY SYSTEM

As illustrated in the chart (Fig. 7), the seven centers are stocked with microfilm copies of periodicals. They are also set up with equipment to make microfiche-to-microfiche duplicate copies quickly and inexpensively.

The user will send his request for information to any of the centers through the proper channels. The center will have the means of finding the proper information in the storage file and will then, using the microfiche-to-microfiche duplicating equipment, produce a film copy for the user.

Duplicate copies of the microfiche can be mailed first class or airmail very economically. Five standard 105 X

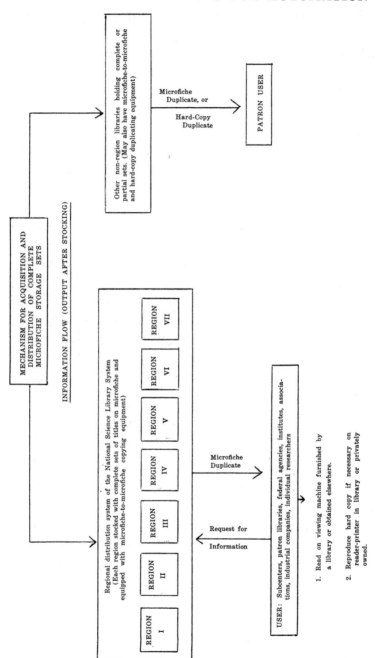

Figure 7.

148-mm microfiches of 8-mil stock plus a substantial mailing envelope weigh one ounce. In the United States, therefore, five microfiches containing 300, 8½ × 11-in. pages could be mailed first class for 5 cents and airmail for 8 cents. Three hundred 8½ × 11-in. pages in original hard copy form weigh over two pounds plus the packing. To mail five microfiches to Europe the cost would be 11 cents by surface mail and 30 cents by airmail. To mail a 300-page book airmail to European countries would cost approximately $4.00.

When the film reaches the ultimate user, there are two ways in which he can use the information:

1. He may refer to the microfiche by enlarging it on a viewing machine.
2. He may produce a hard copy print of any or all frames from the microfiche.

In many cases, reference to the microfiche on a viewing machine is adequate and in other cases there may be a requirement for hard copy for a few or all of the frames included in the microfiche.

If hard copy is needed, printout equipment such as a reader-printer would be required. Our discussion is on the basis of providing the facilities and making hard copy at the point of use which means: the subcenter, patron library, industrial company office, and, in some cases, in the home or office of the individual user.

The microfiche itself is quite inexpensive and may be retained as part of a personal file or subject file which may be built up in this form, or it may be thrown away after it has served its purpose.

Depending on the material and quantities used, the cost of the microfiche duplicates, for materials only, is estimated in a range from 6 to 15 cents per microfiche.

Equipment

All of the equipment necessary to start this program is available at the present time for purchase off-the-shelf. Although it is hoped that more and better equipment is in the offing, this equipment now in existence would make it possible to inaugurate and operate the program outlined in Dr. Warren's report.

The equipment now exists to produce microfiche of excellent quality in large quantities at reasonable prices for the production of the master and the copies with which to stock the centers.

Microfiche readers are available at reasonable costs.

Several reader-printers are on the market and these will do the job at reasonable costs.

There are a few portable readers on the market which can be moved from location to location or used in the homes or offices of individuals. It is likely that additional portable equipment (hopefully at cost low enough to permit wide individual ownership) will become available.

There are libraries other than the centers which may buy all or part of the microfiche that will be placed in the centers. In this case it would be possible for these libraries to equip themselves to make microfiche-to-microfiche copies for their patrons. Equipment now exists to do this job and is available at less than $1,000.


CONCLUSION

This discussion on the use of microforms in the proposed National Science Library System has been presented in order to examine various factors relating to stocking of the system with the periodicals to be included.

We have discussed various microforms and the mechanisms for their use. We have presented microfiche as possibly the most appropriate medium for use in the National Science Library System after taking into consideration the matters of production, standards, costs and space.

There are obviously other problems relating to other segments of Dr. Warren's proposal. However, my task has been really to establish the fact that it is possible now, within the present state of the art, to stock the system with information through the use of microforms, and to disseminate the information to the user.

# CHAPTER 3

# THE INFLUENCE OF AUTOMATION ON THE DESIGN OF A UNIVERSITY LIBRARY

ANDREW D. OSBORN

*Professor, Graduate School of Library*

*and Information Sciences*

*University of Pittsburgh*

## INTRODUCTION

The May 1964 issue of the *Architectural Forum* carried an article entitled "Buildings for Books—Are They Obsolete?" The very title reflects the theme of this conference to a greater, or one may hope, to a lesser degree. The extreme position must be faced for the simple reason that it has been made operative at Grand Valley State College where the bookstock has been limited to 23,000 volumes and even these were looked on as nothing more than a concession to the sentimentality of the faculty. The proponent of this radical change in college-library planning and design is Sol Cornberg who has been called "perhaps the most radical prophet of the new library technology." To him books are inefficient. This is what he says:

It's not that we don't like them—my wife is a novelist as a matter of fact—but they just aren't the best way to transmit information anymore. We don't like the laborious problems of finding information in them. Furthermore, to serve a thousand students you need multiple copies. You need storage space for them. The weight of the books is reflected in the architectural costs. Floors get heavier, steel supports, foundations get heavier. Yet in a cabinet the size of my desk or a bit higher we can store 20,000 volumes on microfilm. Nobody can tear a page out of them. They don't smell of old vellum or glue, but you can browse through them and sit there and read them.

Behind this theorizing—surely "philosophy" would be an inappropriate term for so antihumanistic a viewpoint —is Cornberg's belief that reading is passing as a primary from of information intake, his belief even that reading and writing will become obsolete skills. Audiovisual techniques replete with films, lectures, and other materials piped into the home will, he feels, lead to better and faster learning, just as today's student is said to learn more easily from a television screen than from a book.

The Grand Valley State College Library was designed for 256 carrels each with a microphone, two loudspeakers, an eight-inch television picture tube, and a telephone dial. Information stored in what is called a "use attitude" will be available in the carrel. In Mr. Cornberg's words:

There will be up to 310 audiotapes—that is, 310 talking books. These will be programmed for self-learning. On a typical day the student would go to his class or laboratory. That is, he would participate in a group learning activity. After his lesson he goes to his carrel for individual learning. There, by simply dialing a code number, he will be able to get a repeat of the lecture, excerpts as they apply to his assigned lesson, a list of problems. He will use the microphone to record his answers on tape, erase and correct them, if necessary, then dial his instructor. He then plays the tape for his instructor.

The outcome of the Grand Valley State College Library experiment will be awaited with great interest; and in the meantime it is probably wise to suspend judgment on Cornberg's dramatic utterance: "My advice is: plan no more buildings for library use. The library space is a concession to the past. Don't invest in bricks and mortar!" One task will obviously consist of attempting to reconcile his thinking with that which went into creation of the Lamont Library at Harvard. There a premium was placed not only on superior learning but also on the stimulation that comes from finding things out for one's self over and above what is required in the basic faculty-student relationship, on honors work of a kind that develops from individual research and reflection—even, one may well go on to say, from the fondness for books which a Lamont or a Houghton Library inculates in so many ways, not the least of which being the use of a hand printing press.

## INFORMATION RETRIEVAL

Audiovisual techniques, then, are one cause for thought; but for the most part these scientific aids to teaching and learning are not belligerent towards libraries in general or towards college libraries in particular. The information-retrieval story is a very different one. From the beginning, with Vannevar Bush's classic paper of 1945 in the *Atlantic Monthly*, a two-pronged attack has been launched: on the one hand, libraries are branded as inept, inefficient; on the other hand, science and the computer represent knights in shining armor, come to the rescue. Writing in the Bush tradition, Professor Kemeny of Dartmouth recently declared that the library as it has existed has virtually run its course and will be obsolete, if not by the year 2000, at least by 2100. Kemeny deplores the minutes it takes to get a book from the shelves or the time it takes to get a book returned from circulation or on interlibrary loan. A footnote in the Library of Congress report on automation carries this impatience to an extreme when it says: "To the reader a delay of more than ⅕ second is sufficiently annoying to reduce the appeal, and hence the use, of the system" that must be devised. One can make a case for high speed in clinical and defense-related situations, but it is hard to justify it in most other instances. Actually much research must be patient; one cannot, for example, master Heidegger's existentialist thought without patient study and a vast amount of reflection; much can be done in the classroom and with audiovisual aids to enable a person to grasp the essence of Heidegger, but in the last analysis it will be the time-consuming study and reading which bring about mastery of his system. Stafford Warren's paper on the proposed National Library of Science takes a more moderate view of service speed; it still wants photocopies to be in the hands of researchers rapidly, not necessarily though at split-second speed. On the other hand, it follows the Bush-Kemeny tradition by speaking of alleged "chaos" in libraries. There is no occasion to damn libraries in order to advance the claims of more sophisticated types of reader service. Actually the problems on both sides are so great that a joining of forces is called for, not a division that finds fault or tries to dispense with the other.

Three positions have to be made clear in considering how far it is possible to go in automating a library. First, there is the possible conversion of various technical processes. Experimental work is going on in these areas, e.g., by converting the shelf list to punched-card form, by testing out the computer for the checking in of current serials, and by utilizing a wide variety of equipment for library charging systems. Nothing conclusive has so far been determined in most of these undertakings. There has been negative evidence as in the work done at the University of Michigan which showed that television consultation of the card catalog, while technically feasible, is impractical; and there has been positive gain in public libraries through being able to end the tedious process known as "slipping books." But for the most part the potential contribution of automation to library operations remains to be seen.

Second, there is the position taken in the recent report on automation in the Library of Congress. The report recommends computerization of the cataloging and reference functions. Equipment to allow for this type of automation (i.e., a computer to handle $10^{12}$ bits) is not now on the market but is confidently expected by 1969, so a start can be made then on the conversion of the L.C. catalog records of various kinds. The aim is to complete the task in 1972. Beyond this the project looks to two future stages: one, the computerized reproduction of tables of contents and other matter to facilitate the selection of items from long printout bibliographies, the other, the computerized reproduction of the full text of all items under bibliographical control. The latter development cannot be anticipated before the turn of the century because it will require a computer capable of handling $10^{14}$ bits; however, it anticipates the third and ultimate goal of IR in which the total system is computerized. In one respect the proposal for a National Library of Science represents an attempt at a total system—that is, insofar as it would comprise both bibliographical control and the relevant texts in a package deal.

Two facts emerge from this analysis. The total system for the Library of Congress cannot be expected before the twenty-first century. But on the other hand, a partial realization of a total system can be forecast either as soon as the proposed National Library of Science becomes operational or by 1969 when the Library of Congress may have begun work on the conversion of its catalog records.

PEACEFUL COEXISTENCE

Already there is a total computerized library in operation. It is known as WALNUT and is in the Central Intelligence Agency. After many years of seeking a solution to the immensely difficult problem of the bibliographical control of intelligence materials, numbered in the millions, IBM has developed a photographic-electronic library system which retrieves bibliographical data in a matter of about five seconds. After selection from the printout bibliography of the documents for perusal, further electronic steps lead to textual printouts at extremely high speed or, if preferred, lead to viewing on a screen.

At the present juncture, however, the concern is not over total systems such as WALNUT but over the proper relationships between libraries and IR. It is noteworthy that while the proposal for a National Library of Science joins the twenty-year-old castigation of libraries, it does not call for their end. Rather, it regards the National Library of Science as a comprehensive way of complementing the work of the scientific and technical library. Its goal is to strengthen existing libraries immeasurably by making the totality of current scientific journals available to them. That totality has tremendous implications from the point of view of bibliographical control; at the same time availability of the text of the journals for photocopy purposes is an enormous, if expensive, enlargement of existing local and national copying services. Were it more than this, were it a full-fledged total system, it would undoubtedly do harm to its own ends for it would cause many a journal to cease publication through loss of subscriptions. It can be appreciated accordingly that the National Library of Science proposal is a moderate one.

From such moderation a great deal of good can result because IR and libraries are each assigned a clear role to play. Their mutual insights can therefore be brought to bear on the task of making the most of the two modes of bibliographical and textual control. This live-and-let-live policy will, on further analysis, prove to be still more desirable because not all library purposes are information directed and accordingly strong candidates for IR techniques. The world of the imagination lies outside the exigencies of the computer to a high degree; so does the world of knowledge for the sake of knowledge, or knowledge for the sake of unsophisticated activities and vocations; so does the world of recreation—and attention to all such noninformation areas is a major concern of libraries. This is another way of saying that IR, all things considered, can justify itself and its great cost principally when sophisticated pressure areas are involved, as can be the case in defense and clinical urgency as well as large-scale government and business enterprises such as census taking, internal-revenue operations, and banking. In many another area application of high-powered, high-cost methods to low-pressure matters can be on the order of dilettantism or boondoggling. These are dangers to be guarded against; so IR should not be regarded as the universal panacea or method that some of its enthusiastic supporters would have it be.

This is far from the first time in history that a new and enterprising discipline has arrogated to itself basic and universal functions. One has only to think back to the similar claims made for psychology in the last quarter of the nineteenth century when even logic and mathematics were interpreted psychologically; and psychology had scarcely settled down when all knowledge had to be interpreted in social-science terms. Claims of this kind tend to be a sign of immaturity; and IR, as an emerging discipline, should guard against the exaggerated pronouncements of its most enthusiastic protagonists, all the more so when big business markets can obscure issues with sales talk. Typical of these statements is the March 1964 issue of *Fortune* which places the computer ahead of all other inventions: the printing press or the wheel, the steam engine or the electric motor, the dynamo or atomic power. It would not be easy to substantiate the case for the computer over the printing press. In specific areas it is more important than Gutenberg's invention; but printing has, and will continue to have, far wider applications; and in many respects it is proper to regard the computer with its printout potential as another form of the printing press—just as on careful analysis the proposal for the National Library of Science is, on the textual side, essentially a superphotocopying service, not a genuine storage of textual matter.

If it can be assumed that IR and library science will set about the delimitation of their areas of responsibility, then one of the most urgent tasks will be the determination of the optimum size of a library collection, either for a closed or an open-access library, to be operated more or less in a traditional manner before IR techniques should take over organizationally. Failure to come to grips with this problem was the most serious defect in the L.C. automation inquiry. As a consequence there is the glaring example in the report of a student edition of *Hamlet* which is to be obtained by activating an expensive computer instead of having it available in an open-access collection or through a card or book catalog, the latter possibly as a by-product of automation. Simple unsophisticated needs such as a student edition of *Hamlet* can represent nothing but an abuse of the computer which ought to be geared to give the scholar the total listing or a specified selection of the *Hamlet* literature. It should be clear that one ought to be able to get quick reference books and basic bookstock with self-service methods—in a library of the year 2000 or 2100—as well as in the library of 1964 or 1969. In one field after another, as diverse as carpentry and aeronautics, we learn to utilize the right equipment, small or large, for any given assignment. Likewise in the library field different methodology has developed for different types and size of library as well as for different reader needs; and this varied methodology is apt to continue into the indefinite future.

## LIMITATIONS OF INFORMATION RETRIEVAL IN THE BOOK FIELD

The argument so far is that a total system is unlikely and unnecessary for most library situations; therefore the objective should be the pooling of IR and library insights, skills, and experience to bring about the desired interplay of the two methodologies. Also in the discussion some areas have been designated as unsuited to IR techniques. Now it is desirable to go a step further and to list some of the limitations of IR in the book field.

Some limitations are those common to any substitute medium, and of course IR would be a substitute medium insofar as it provided textual coverage. In many research situations first-class work is done with originals rather than copies, no matter how fine those copies may be. There are very notable exceptions to this rule; in particular the major part of the nonhistorical sciences constitute exceptions. But for the rest we have for long needed a full-scale study by a bibliographer, such as William A. Jackson, to bring out the limitations of photocopies, invaluable aids to research and scholarship as they are. Today's researcher and scholar are fortunate in having these aids. When the library of Professor Kittredge was bequeathed to Harvard, it was sad to observe the notebooks into which he had patiently copied in longhand pamphlet after pamphlet in the British Museum. Currently such a scholar could use the originals and then have photocopies made, in effect editing them for his later use: for the typical photocopy is an un-edited version which in certain situations can leave much to be desired. Some of the situations are:

1. The dating of a manuscript, sometimes of a rare book, can be done far better from the original than from any copy.

2. Textual interpretation of a book or manuscript commonly depends on access to an original, e.g., because the typography in itself can tell a story.

3. The Yale facsimile of the Shakespeare first folio, for which a considerable number of "typographical errors" have been noted, makes it clear that even the very best of reproductions may leave much to be desired.

4. In some outstanding art libraries, reproductions of the works of artists are deliberately cataloged under the compiler or the title, rather than under the artist, because even the best of reproductions cannot be equated with the actual work of the artist.

5. Manuscript additions to a book or manuscript may be difficult to interpret adequately from a copy: to tell, for example, whether the writing is in a contemporary or later hand.

6. Erasures, as well as words that have been inked out, cannot be determined from a copy whereas there are techniques for restoring such deletions when the original is in hand.

7. Cancels in rare books and substitute leaves in manu-scripts cannot be detected from photocopies.

8. Color is often significant for art, botany, geography, medicine, and other disciplines; while color reproductions are possible, the great mass of photo-copies ignores color, just as the computer does.

In certain fields the difference between a photocopy and an original can result in undistinguished work as against first-class scholarship. Our university libraries have a definite responsibility to provide the materials which will permit scholars to undertake first-class work. If points such as the ones given above were not so, there would be no occasion for a scholar to go to the Huntington, the British Museum, the Bibliothèque Nationale: for photocopies of their holdings would otherwise suffice. The libraries that attract the largest numbers of visiting scholars are those which have original editions and manuscripts, which have distinguished copies of one kind or another. In the latter category, for example, if one were working on the German poet Stefan George it would be a case of going to the Houghton Library at Harvard for the extensively annotated copies and manuscripts of the late Professor Vietor, the great authority on George.

All of these limitations of photocopies apply equally to the computer as a storer and reproducer of actual texts. And to these limitations it is necessary to add that there are certain types of information that even a multi-million IR system would not answer. For instance, the English Department at Smith College wanted to know the source of the long Latin quotation which occurs between Acts 1 and 2 of Eugene O'Neill's *Strange Interlude*. It was tracked down in the New York Public Library by the device of taking the most uncommon word in the quotation and checking it in the great German dictionary which attempts to cite every use of Latin words. The quotation turned up at the very end of thousands of citations because it was from a medieval work. Or, again, the scholar at work on an attempt to date the *Second Shepherd's Play* would never expect a computer to make the jump from the shepherd's gift of a tennis ball to Henderson's list, published at the back of a sporting book, of the earliest use of the word "tennis." The list itself might be on the computer, but it is too much to expect that the vocabulary of the play would be.    Such examples could be multiplied many times over at reference desks where the skill of the librarian calls on a kind of sixth sense to make associations and run down apparently unobtainable information.

## HUMANISTIC VALUES IN THE AGE OF THE SCIENTIFIC REVOLUTION

It has already been pointed out that information is only one of the functions of a library, at least as far as school, public, and college libraries are concerned. The noninformational functions should expand greatly in the years ahead as leisure time increases and as the scientific revolution takes deeper hold. One can carry the matter further and say that in a machine age it is undesirable to have to do even a major share of one's reading on a screen, let alone all of it. For one thing that would mean too much regimentation, too much having to work where the machines are instead of being able to read in the office, at home, in the open air, on a plane, etc. And it is common today for the researcher and scholar to turn to recreational forms of reading to get away from the concentration of study and work. Thus Professor Kittredge was a great reader of detective stories; so was Professor Reisner, the Egyptologist, whose great collection of detective stories was shipped from Cairo to Boston on his death. Very often the reading a professional man gets from a public library in itself could appear strange; his professional reading being done elsewhere, he turns to the public library for works of the imagination, recreational and avocational reading, and so on.

One further point.  Several decades ago the librarian of the Clements Library in Ann Arbor wrote an article on librarians as the enemies of books, and IR specialists should be on their guard to avoid a similar charge. The book often has an esthetic value in and for itself; it can have other values because of the associations, scarcity, or worth. We go back to old books as old friends. The collector, like the rare-book librarian, gets pleasure from both the running down of a new find and the constant consultation of earlier acquisitions. The printout, for all its value as a tool of research, will never have the same appeal; in fact the printout to a high degree is looked on as expendable; it is not to be collected and preserved; and one would scarcely take a keen delight in a library of printouts were one to be made. This attitude of mind can be called sentimentality, just as the 23,000 volumes at Grand Valley State College are set down to sentimentality on the part of the faculty; but after all the values we know are human values, not machine values. It is extremely important to preserve every single humanistic element in an age of science, in a machine age.

## APPLICATION TO THE DESIGN OF UNIVERSITY LIBRARIES

The foregoing arguments were necessary to any discussion of possible effects on the design of university-library buildings. Their review is desirable because for some time librarians have been hesitating over the extent to which automation may at any moment call for radical departures from existing practice; and despite all the flexibility that goes into a present-day library building, it is not beyond the realm of possibility that one could make serious miscalculations. Already the design of library buildings has become a great specialty, so much so that a library consultant is almost a necessity. But even the consultant may be in the dark as can be seen from the observation of Keyes Metcalf quoted by Alvin Toffler: "We have no idea how far audio-visual can go in the next few years, and it is therefore foolish to put up audio-visual buildings as such. The new library can give it space for the next five years, until we know more about how far it will go in higher education."

The history of library architecture remained very much of a constant from Roman times to the end of the nineteenth century when the introduction of steel made it possible to get away once and for all from the wall storage of books. Since that revolutionary change developments of all kinds have followed rapidly on the heels of one another, not the least of them being the rejection of the idea of a multipurpose main university library which was occasioned by the highly successful system of annexes built around the Widener Library at Harvard.

In addition to being well versed in all points of historical development and the reasons for them, the university-library planner of today must be thoroughly well informed on a multiplicity of technical matters, many of which found no place in Blanche McCrum's list of items for a college library building which she compiled just a generation ago. How technical a modern library can be may be inferred from the fact that 12 percent or more of the total building cost can be for the electrical and electronic aspects alone, while if air-conditioning is added on the figure may rise to 25 percent. Allowance must be made nowadays for all manner of equipment such as the following:

Adding machines
Cove lighting, exhibition-case lighting, general illumination including, on occasion, luminous ceilings
Electric door locks
Electric typewriters and erasers
Elevators with memory boards
Emergency lighting and an emergency source of current
Fire-alarm systems
Microfilm cameras for acquisition and other purposes
Microfilm, microcard, and microprint readers and even printers

Music and language listening facilities of various kinds
Pasting machines
Photographic laboratory
Postage meters
Telephones
Xerox and other copying machines, even to the extent of a
    Copyflo which the Widener Library at Harvard found necessary
    and had great difficulty getting into the building

Now to all these technical matters—to say nothing of the difficulty of guessing the size of the student body in the next ten or twenty-five years—comes the big question mark of the effect of the computer on university-library design. The following points are relevant.

1. Should the National Library of Science eventuate as a computerized record, the impact will not be on main university libraries so much as on departmental libraries in the fields of science and technology—that is, unless it should prove desirable to establish a National Library of Science outpost in the main library or establish the intake point there. Rather generally, however, one would prefer, for geographical and other reasons, to locate the new medium in the science precincts of the university. It is reasonable to say, therefore, that a main university-library building would be left relatively unaffected by this aspect of IR.

2. There would be a strong argument in favor of a major consolidation of departmental libraries in the area of science and technology in order to take full advantage of the new service. So the big impact of a computerized National Library of Science would be on the planning and organization of science-library buildings or areas of buildings.

3. The means of communication with the nearest National Library of Science branch would have a major bearing on (1) and (2). If short-wave or coaxial-cable connections were possible, a network could be established

very desirably not only within a university-library system but also with other science libraries in the vicinity.

4. Almost surely the system would have to be based on printout facilities because reading at a distance would require far too many outlets to be feasible. Also the print-out circuit could operate in most instances quite satisfactorily from midnight to early morning, a period when transmission lines would be less in demand for competing services.

5. Apart from such major and expensive developments as the L.C. automation program and the National Library of Science, library catalogs should not operate through computers. The next phase of library catalogs should be the book form. These can to advantage be produced with the aid of computers; but by and large the book catalog will prove to be far more effective all around the campus than will the computer-type catalog proposed for the Library of Congress. Actual computer catalogs could well develop in certain department libraries, however.

6. For acquisition the greatest gain would come from the computerization of publishers' stock records. Now it is difficult and wasteful of time to try to determine whether a work is in print or not; and frequently, when *Books in Print* lists an item as available, a report comes back from the publisher that the book is out of print. A computerized publishers' record would give the day-by-day story as items go out of stock or come back into print.

7. For serial control records commercial publishers at least could include the coding for use at a computerized serial checklist.

8. The Library of Congress is seeking an automated catalog card. Should that eventuate in any form, it would then be possible to automate much of the cataloging process in a university library.

9. Much work will be necessary before computerized circulation records can be contrived satisfactorily and relatively inexpensively.

10. It is a shock to the librarian as a book collector to spend ten or twenty million dollars or more on a new library building; his great desire is to have such a sum for the development of the collections which would really benefit from financing on so large a scale. The same comparison must be made with the cost of IR; a truly great collection could be built up if the amount of money that goes into IR could go into the acquisition of books.

11. In general wiring on a somewhat more liberal scale than in the past should be provided in the construction of main and departmental libraries. In particular, wiring should be provided for carrels around the periphery, perhaps even for all carrels. Apart from this the amount of space for AV or IR intake will not be so great that the current degree of flexibility in design will not provide for future developments.

12. Microfilm should increasingly be favored over microcards and microprint since it is the most convenient form for transmission by shortwave or coaxial cable.

13. A storage library of tremendous capacity will be an absolute necessity in every university library; much ingenuity will probably have to go into its organization to permit it to carry a greater and greater proportion of the total library bookstock.

14. Apart from the storage library, decentralization of university-library collections will have to proceed at an accelerated pace. Eventually the main bookstock would be devoted only to certain of the humanities and social sciences, all other topics going to departmental libraries; and even the residue in the main bookstock would be subject to constant transfer to the storage library. In such ways Professor Kemeny's prediction that a library of over 10,000,000 is an impossible conglomeration would

prove to be false; and as long as no unit other than the storage library were to grow indefinitely in size, such a collection of collections would be practicable far into the future.

15. The monolith of the past may well cease to be the goal of university-library architecture. A massing of structures may develop instead, the alternative being a series of annexes clustered around the central collection. Actually the items (13)–(15) can be anticipated with or without automation; sheer size will force such developments.

16. In short, university libraries of the year 2000 or 2100 will look very much like the newer libraries of today. They will be more complex in their organization because the bookstock will be greatly splintered, because they will be interconnected nationally with other repositories, and because they will even more than today rely on a multitude of forms, including AV and TV devices, over and above the microforms and other nonbook materials now available.

17. More radical changes will take place in department-library design than in the planning of main libraries. Especially affected will be the department libraries in science and technology. Not only will they draw on national services such as the National Library of Science but in some instances a total system is possible.

18. The cost of the future library need not be a deterrent, as Professor Kemeny fears. Machlup has pointed out that the dollar value of knowledge-production has to be interpreted in the light of the total national product; and in any event he would regard a library as a "social investment."

## CONCLUSION

The general finding has to be that IR will not radically change the basic design and size of main university-library buildings even though it can lead to substantial changes in potentially high pressure departmental libraries such as those for science and technology. Quite clearly, IR adds a new dimension to established university-library programs in just the same way that all developments in the communications field have added to the cumulative total without replacing one another. First came the manuscript, then the printed page; and to them have been added from the 1930's on, microprint of all kinds, AV in varied forms, and finally the computer with its printouts. So the university library of the future, in the year 2000 or 2100, can be anticipated as a still more sophisticated complex of the traditional book-stock plus AV, plus IR. And this means in particular: (1) an intensification of the trend towards individual accommodations such as wired carrels; (2) all conceivable wiring and equipment for technical processes as well as reader services; (3) planned, coordinated, and continuing decentralization of the collections; (4) expanding storage-library accommodations, whether cooperative or not; (5) a computer-based book catalog, both local and cooperative in character, such as will make it possible for the processing staff to be located at a distance from the public-service areas and probably in another building altogether; and (6) intensive research on the methodology of the multimillion-volume library, especially on how to make selfservice methods increasingly effective, in part through classification systems designed to facilitate open-access work.

PART II

DISCUSSION OF WORKING PAPERS

# CHAPTER 4

# DISCUSSION RELATING TO
# DR. WARREN'S PAPER

Stafford L. Warren

It gives me great pleasure to present a proposal for discussion to such a sophisticated group as this—particularly a proposal to employ computerized techniques in a National Library of Science System and network. While I can in no sense be called a computer buff, I have had a rather extensive contact with many aspects of this problem in the biomedical and campus libraries over the last five years as the former Dean of Medicine and Vice-Chancellor of the Health Sciences at the University of California at Los Angeles.

During this time a large-scale campus effort was developing in data processing so that when the new School of Library Sciences came into full bloom on that campus, advantage was taken of the new faculty and know-how to develop a curriculum and do research in computerizing library techniques. The efforts at first were directed toward the life and biological sciences, but these efforts could not be restricted and have spread quickly to all of the sciences. Close contact was made with the developments in the Federal agencies and particularly with those in MEDLARS; in fact, one of the Medical Faculty, Dr. N. Brill, was a Regent of the National Library of Medicine.

The problem is not restricted alone to the tremendous expansion required by the University of California to build and equip so many new campus libraries and a new biomedical library almost every five years for new medical centers. The expansion is nationwide. Not only is the literature expanding but so are the graduate student rosters and faculty who produce this swelling mass of material and are, at the same time, its users. Existing libraries face stack expansions for which there is no space and new libraries are at a loss as to what their future stacks might be.

There has been almost no discussion of the physical and structural problems of libraries. Most of the reports and discussion have been directed toward the problems created by the growing size and complexity of the published literature, the complexity of dealing with government reports, the methods for summarizing the literature, the possibilities of prepublication communication of new findings, and so on.

The proposal which I will discuss is now in administrative channels as a response to those recommendations of the 1962 President's Panel Report on Mental Retardation which urged that improvements be made in the accessibility of research information to the scientist. The Panel pointed out that no field of science should be excluded and that computer techniques be exploited for library purposes. The proposal will be screened by the Office of Science and Technology and the Bureau of the Budget before going to the President and, I hope, to Congress, where its merits and demerits can be openly debated and proper legislation and budget provided for implementation.

For a year or more I have explored the library resources, policies, programs, responsibilities, needs and trends both in the Federal, private and commercial or industrial sectors. During this time I have had the benefit of numerous reports and conferences and consultations with many thoughtful and sophisticated individuals from many disciplines, institutions and agencies. These have been too numerous to credit with any one segment of the proposal which gradually evolved as the discussions proceeded. I am convinced that the time is ripe for a development of the sort proposed here and of this magnitude, particularly if it can be carried out in several steps. It will benefit all scientists as well as those in the limited field of mental retardation.

As a result of my survey there has emerged what I believe to be the simplest way of taking the first step. It preserves what already exists.

In principle it is proposed to create a computer-based pool of tapes and microform which are contributed by the Federal and other libraries or contractors from their own or assigned holdings in the scientific literature.

Once the contributions are in proper form, the total holding is replicated into the seven or more regional centers, from which a subnet is formed for distribution to university libraries and other users in amounts required and requested for their purposes.

Since there must be a beginning, I have chosen the published scientific journal literature as the initial vehicle. It is the open literature where the truth can be defended or attacked. It is a specific, compact and discrete segment of the literature readily demonstrated to anyone and particularly to Congress. It is the part of the literature most used by scholars and advanced students.

Most large professional groups already have standing committees working on a glossary or thesaurus in their field. This fact offers an opportunity for coordination and the establishment of compatibility of standards. National conferences are needed to work out agreements on standards.

An additional specialist group will have to be created to carry out the new service in the libraries of the country. The educational program to train these personnel must be created in existing or new schools of library science on an urgent basis. I believe that such a program should include additional offerings in English (semantics) and philosophy (logic) as well as in programming and electronics; thus leading to the strengthening of the faculties in university departments not likely to gain research and educational support from other granting agencies.

Pilot studies and research in methodology are required. Fortunately the whole theory of computer techniques permits great flexibility so that conversion from one system to another is possible during the trial period of the first two years or even later.

MEDLARS of the National Library of Medicine has shown great potential in the first computer printout of the *Index Medicus*. While it should be considered experimental it has proven the feasibility of these first steps; namely, to handle the citations of the medical-biological literature which it contains.

As the art becomes more sophisticated it is believed that shortly abstracts and facsimiles could be handled efficiently as well. Books, manuscripts and other types of communication can be dealt with separately and at a later date.

Because of its advanced experience it is recommended that MEDLARS be expanded physically and that the housekeeping for the system remain with the U. S. Public Health Service. The Advisory Council device and the Advisory Committee on Operations are designed to cope with the funding and administrative details to create, organize and operate the system.

I have not spelled out many details which may be changed by what happens in the debate during the hearings on the legislation or by experience as the program develops.

At this point, I need your comments, if you wish to make them, about the possible usefulness of such a system for your library situation. To be useful in my discussions with the Office of Science and Technology and the Congress, I will need them as soon as possible.

Allen Kent
*(as Chairman)*

Dr. Warren's proposal for a National Science Library system has been presented to the participants as a working paper. Dr. Warren's amplifying remarks have provided an overview with regard to three of the problems that will have to be solved in order to get a program such as this rolling.

*First,* involving the control of the source materials themselves.

*Second,* the creation of standards to permit consistent analysis in an operating system.

*Third,* providing enough people to man the libraries in the proposed new system.

As I interpret his remarks and the paper he presented, he has given a broad-brush treatment of the system and said, in effect, "Let's stop arguing, if we agree in principle, and let's start worrying about doing the job." We have an unusual opportunity here to start considering this proposal. Before we go any further, I would like to ask for questions relating to Dr. Warren's presentation or anything relating to the basic plan.

Question*

I have gone over your paper several times to try to pinpoint whether you are going to cover technology and engineering. It is called a library of science. Would you define the term *science?* Would you comment whether you mean engineering, the engineering science library, the NASA, AEC, and DDC information centers?

---

*In a few cases, it was not possible to identify from the transcription a participant who posed a question. These questions are identified as above.

### Stafford L. Warren

I have said the published scientific and professional journals; this includes everything, the physical sciences, engineering; it includes everything. I couldn't leave out the behavioral sciences or art because recreational and music therapy are very important in the training of the retarded. By designating a professional society and its published journal we get everything except the textbook, and what is in published volumes. We have had to leave them out, because the art is not sophisticated enough at the moment to include them along with all of the rest. Later on they might be.

I would like to start with the published journals, because mostly they have associations behind them. They have the power and capacity and individuals to produce the glossary. They have a gate through which all the publications are inspected and moderated; namely, the editor and the editorial staff, and the material is in the open literature for all to see and to debate. This is something you can give to a Congressman and say that this is the kind of material that gets put in the computer system first as a title and as an author; and as we get more and more sophisticated, then abstracts and, later, the article itself. A technical journal would be included if it subscribes to the glossary and editorial policy.

### Question

Are you planning to go down to the trade journal?

### Stafford L. Warren

This would be a question that the committee on operations which after all is made up of librarians, would have to decide. It would have to be decided on the basis of the use to be made of it. Who are the customers? Scientists? Technologists? I don't know where you stop. This is the problem that faces every librarian today. It would still face this system. The system eventually would have almost an unlimited capacity and could accept anything in the way of new information in any form. There is some comment that journals will disappear. I don't think they will for a long, long time. It represents your professional colleagues; it is something close at hand that you can receive regularly, look at personally, have on your desk, and take home at night rather than get a printout from a computer. There is a lot more to help you in a journal: to browse in, and to think in other channels.

## Question

Your definition of science is very broad.

## Stafford L. Warren

The definition is accordinng to the dictionary. It is the regular compilation and analysis of information—any systematized collection of knowledge.

## Edward M. Heiliger

During the past four years the library profession has been working with the Library of Congress on their planning for automation. A report on this planning was published recently. There is a marked similarity between that report and yours. Most libraries are interested in all fields, rather than just the sciences. Actually, the social sciences and the humanities have traditionally made more demands on libraries than the sciences. Therefore, the possibility of the Library of Congress developing such a plan has more appeal than an organization devoted exclusively to the sciences. Inasmuch as we are all involved in the activities of the Library of Congress and have always looked to the Library of Congress for leadership in national library matters, I would like to have you talk a little more about your plan as it relates to the Library of Congress. Before leaving the Library of Congress, I would like to add that we all make use of the National Union Catalog which it publishes.

I would also like to have your comment on the adaptability of the computer system being used by the MEDLARS Project, to the more accessible computer systems that are available around the country. The Honeywell computer being used at the National Library of Medicine is a rare "bird." The most accessible computers around the country are IBM and I would like to raise the question of compatibility. Finally, I would question using Veterans Administration facilities. The VA seems to be closely related to politics and I would be worried about the stability of any arrangement with it.

## Stafford L. Warren

May I say that you will notice only two relationships for the veterans: one is the site, the land, because of its juxtaposition with medical schools and universities; the second is that the VA has one of the largest integrated biomedical library systems in the nation. There is another advantage too.

There is a contract underway now to convert the MEDLARS Honeywell tapes for use in an IBM system. The VA has a lot of this equipment which was installed for actuarial purposes. It can be used for this purpose. There also are a lot of universities who already have computer equipment so that the biomedical net can be spread in a small way very soon.

I go back to the statement that MEDLARS is an experiment on a large scale. At this stage no one knows how applicable it would be. However, it clearly demonstrates the feasibility of the use of computers in producing citations and an index. I don't see why we couldn't start another one right beside it with a different program and try them both out, or even four or five systems, in the first two years of this program, in order to find out just where we stand.

The Library of Congress is in the legislative branch, and therefore is vulnerable to budgetary difficulties and it has no organization to fight for its needs.

Several reports have recommended that it be transferred to the Executive Branch, but for a variety of reasons this has never been brought about. I recommend that the new system be set up in the Executive Branch somewhere. It could be a new commission which the Bureau of the Budget doesn't like to contemplate, because a new commissioner means a whole new organization probably with little or no experience. There are several operating agencies in the government that can do this. MEDLARS happens to be on its way, and its computer sophistication is quite important. The democratic and administrative traditions built up by the NIH Advisory Councils and study sections in developing new fields of research lend themselves admirably to the development contemplated for the library sciences.

The Library of Congress is in an enviable position to participate by furnishing the material in the humanities and the behavioral sciences. It has the whole field of law, in which the Library of Congress is preeminent and which needs reorganization badly. Its Advisory Committee recommended that the Library of Congress utilize a computer for its catalog. This would be a good start, but will take several years to become implemented. Sooner or later every large library will use computerized techniques. It's only another step then to hook in with the distribution net of the proposed National Library of Science System. Except for the Library of Congress, most of the librarians express interest and a willingness to participate. Of course, I cannot gauge their private reservations at this stage of our discussions.

## Horace Magoun

The brilliant synthesis which Dr. Warren has presented and the scope of his proposed plan is striking, even to those of us who have known before of his great planning ability. The topic of Federal organization is certainly of great relevance to any national program in this field. The discussion has emphasized the patchwork way in which much of our Federal activity has developed in the science library field. We have a library without a scientific agency in the case of the Library of Congress. We have an agency with a related library in the case of the National Institutes of Health and the National Library of Medicine, both of which are components of the United States Public Health Service. We also have an agency without a library in the case of the National Science Foundation. Dr. Warren has emphasized that his proposed National Science Library Network is planned to include all of the sciences—physical, social, and biomedical—and, to my knowledge, the National Science Foundation is the only Federal agency with this range of mandate in its charter.

Dr. Warren has called attention, however, to the value of developing his proposed plan in relation to the enterprising National Library of Medicine, whose MEDLARS program has already begun activity in this direction; as well as to the Veterans Administration hospitals, whose geographic distribution throughout the country is an attractive feature. I would enjoy hearing more of Dr. Warren's thinking about the organizational side of his plan, which is of obvious relevance if this is to be a Federal program.

## Stafford L. Warren

Well, I had several very important dilemmas in that particular direction. The National Science Foundation has had the authority since 1958 in the National Defense Education Act to do something like this, but the National Science Foundation has never adopted the policy of being an operating agency. They wanted to continue as a granting agency. During the year in which I have been thinking and talking to people in this area, it may be that, with a new director, the policy of the National Science Foundation has changed, but I have no evidence of it; and I was informed last year about this time as long as the National Science Foundation was represented in the proposal and could continue its support of the basic sciences in research and education, that this was to be its main role. On the other hand, almost any operating agency in government that has a library at all could do this with a legislative change in its assignment and authority and an appropriate budget. The easiest, of course, is to change the assignment of the National Library of Medicine.

You recall, perhaps last year at this time or earlier, there was quite a bit of discussion about the Institute of Learning. Now if you are to sit back in a smoke-filled room and say how you would like the government to be reorganized you would do something quite different with the Office of Education. It has up to now been essentially the representative of the teachers of primary and secondary schools. It has not responded at all to graduate education.  This not so inconsistent as it might seem at first, because you remember, not longer than ten or fifteen years ago, research was considered to be a luxury item in universities and the universities did not plan for research space nor did they allot faculty time for research; and it is only more recently that the graduate programs have become really strong and emphasized, chiefly because of Federal research support. Commissioner Keppel of the Office of Education and I have discussed this, particularly in view of the fact that the library construction bills in support of educational institutions have passed. There are funds for libraries now for the first time, but these are not directed toward research libraries but libraries in general. My political advisers suggest that it would be impractical politically to try to reorganize education and recreate the Institute of Learning or something allied to it. Mr. Keppel would like very much to strengthen the graduate programs, particularly in the humanities and arts. I think you will find in the ensuing months and years that the whole field of learning will have a new look from his point of view. He is having troubles, because to change the direction of emphasis in a large department in the government is not an easy task.

Joseph Kuney

The heart of the MEDLARS system is primarily designed to alert medical scientists to the available literature. You envision that the National Library of Science would also perform some sort of alerting service?

Stafford L. Warren

Every Federal library has some kind of alerting service now. Once a pool were established, this alerting service could have more comprehensive coverage. Indexing and bibliographic services should continue unless there is some reason for them to die out, such as a change in the interest of the consumer. The National Library of Medicine would continue to ask the MEDLARS to furnish it the *Index Medicus*. Other libraries would ask for their material which they now supply to special customers. Either the pool would print it out for them or the library would use its own computer to arrange and print out the material in a special form to suit its customers. I don't see any reason why the existing indexing, abstracting, clearing houses, information and referral services couldn't grow considerably. They would be more nearly complete in their special services to their users. Each of them has a special discipline or field to cover. It's too big for anyone to do the whole job. In the case of *Chemical Abstracts*, it seems to me that the subsidy just changes. The subsidy would now come in the provision of the "pool," because the authors from zero time on would be required to abstract their own articles and *Chemical Abstracts*, for instance, would have a much better coverage from the pool.

Horace Magoun

Dr. Warren, had you made any public presentation of your plan before this morning?

Stafford L. Warren

No, this is the first time. Prior to this, hearings have been held by the Federal Advisory Council of the Office of Science and Technology. They have appointed a special Task Force to study and recommend. This is the first opportunity I have had to have a professional and academic look at it, so I would like searching questions and also criticism. I had some good advice from my consultant from the staff of the Office of Education and from MEDLARS and individuals in many other agencies, but I don't know that I have got all the loopholes covered. I don't expect to solve all of the problems but have recommended what I believe to be the simplest approach to an organization and funds which could make a start and also deal with these problems as they arise.

CHAPTER **5**

# DISCUSSION RELATING TO
# MR. FREEDMAN'S PAPER

Allen Kent
*(as Chairman)*

"A long journey," to use an old saw, "starts with the first step;" and in looking at the National Science Library System perhaps I was searching for the first step that could be taken that is technologically feasible today, that is economically feasible also, and that has some chance of being acceptable to the library planners throughout the country. It seemed to me that such a first step might involve the control of the source materials by putting them in some form to render them readily reproducible. Mr. Freedman of the Micro Photo Division of Bell & Howell kindly agreed to look at this first step. He presented the background and economics in the report that was distributed (Chapter 2).

*(Here followed a summary of Chapter 2 by Mr. Freedman.)*

Allen Kent

Mr. Freedman, what are the costs of preparing a full size copy from a microfiche (as a single image) as compared with producing a copy of a page directly from a book or periodical?

Samuel B. Freedman

They should be very little different. A microimage can be projected on "reader-printer" equipment for approximately the same cost as getting a copy from the original book or periodical on an office copier.

## Gustave A. Harrer

I don't know exactly how to make this question simple. It certainly is "thinking small," but I am afraid that university librarians are forced to face the problem of cost. I think we are talking about two things in the proposal: one is a possibility of the rather complete bibliographic search for data on a given subject. We might presume, I think, that any project in a large enough corporation or university would have some funds and could afford to pay for searches at centers. The other side of it, though, is this business of storage of materials and, as Mr. Freedman said, we are talking about getting full copies of these materials in microform. I immediately run up against the faculty's great aversion to being forced to use any major amount of material in microform. It seems then that I am faced with the question of duplicating part in hard copy, and storing part of it in microform. I am a bit worried about where I would be able to find the money. In some way I feel I have to make a budgetary switch here. I am going to have to switch money on one side in order to afford the other, and I am not quite sure how to go about this. Is the copy going to be immediately available—and how quickly—from another source? If I didn't have a full micro-form copy, could I get a copy of an individual article from a center? Would the delay be so great that I would have to have my own microfilm copy of anything to take advantage of the system? It is in this general area of making the stuff itself available that I have doubts. If I were to cut out some of the lesser used subscriptions and depend on a microfilm copy, can I then quickly get copies of this from a center or will I have to have my own copy?

## Samuel B. Freedman

This is a good question and I believe it goes directly to the central purpose of Dr. Warren's proposal.

First, let me say that it would not be necessary for you to make any changes in your present periodical program. Under these conditions you could supplement your holdings by using the serv- ices of the closest National Science Library Center, thus ex- panding the amount of material available to the patrons of your library.

Second, you may find it possible to eliminate from your shelves certain periodical holdings which are infrequently used.

For example, you might decide to eliminate certain titles which are over five years old, retaining original copies on your shelves for the latest five-year period. You may find that certain titles can be eliminated entirely because they are infrequently used and because these titles are available on call from the National Science Library System.

Third, you may decide to purchase all of the titles or some of the titles available in the microform through the National Science Library System which is proposed.

Although I respect your comment that certain members of the faculty may prefer to use hard copy rather than a microimage on a reader screen, I believe it is true that people are accepting this type of reference increasingly today. Furthermore, with reader-printer equipment available it is possible to get inexpensive hard copy promptly from the microforms. I believe a system could be set up at the National Science Library Centers so that prompt and inexpensive service would be available where hard copy or microforms are requested.

## John H. Moriarty

In the name of all the scientific editors who sweated and risked bankruptcy for the sake of color in journal articles, are we going to wash that all out now? The Defense Department has been, up to now, dominated by the mathematicians and physicists and engineers to whom color means very little, but this isn't the end of science by any manner or means; and color is necessary for future science. Color is also important in other disciplines. Now I hope, Dr. Warren, it never gets back to Purdue that I am to decide what files are to be kept or I'd never have been allowed off the airplane. The faculty decides these matters and I can't imagine some of our botanists or some of our physiologists letting me off the hook with regard to keeping the original. Even these would fill up my library. Let's just assume now, that I am a university librarian who doesn't give a hoot about costs. If you'd describe the potential of color copying for such material I'd like to hear about it.

## Samuel B. Freedman

It is possible to produce color in the microforms commercially. We are doing this today. The high cost of color has been considered a problem but since Dr. Moriarty does not consider this an objection I will be glad to follow suit.

## John H. Moriarty

If the men need it, there is money.

## Samuel B. Freedman

There are two problem areas with color. First, color is not considered permanent and over the years will probably show some deterioration. The second problem is that color films on the market today do not resolve as well as black and white. This is not a problem as a rule with photographs, but it can be a problem with "Line" work, particularly at the ratios commonly used in microfilming. We have seen evidence that progress is being made in the resolving power of color films. Having raised these possible objections, we believe there is a place for color film, as it is today, in the microforms, and it is possible to produce it commercially where the application exists.

## John H. Moriarty

There is a nice balance between price and storage.

## Samuel B. Freedman

Yes.

## Edward M. Heiliger

I was wondering about this 10 million figure. I have been doing a little figuring here: 2,500 journals for 50 years at 300 pages a year comes to, in my figuring, 37,500,000 pages.

## Allen Kent

The thought was that this would be the *annual* input.

## Edward M. Heiliger

I see; that makes a difference.

## Gustave A. Harrer

This brings up this question of cost. I have made a rough calculation which may be valid. Let us assume that a large university library takes 10,000 periodicals a year. If you could store in film 5,000 of these perhaps not available now, but through a central filming service, one would save on subscription cost about $6.00 per title. This would be $30,000 a year which would be available to reinvest in film. Additionally, if my calculations are right, it would save approximately $9,000 a year in space at $37 a foot in construction cost and so on, so that you come up with almost $40,000 a year to play around with in reinvestment in film, which is a very nice amount. Now how far this would get you in film I don't know, based on 5,000 periodical subscriptions.

### Samuel B. Freedman

In Figure 2-6 (Chapter 2) there is a discussion of costs. You will notice that if 100 libraries would subscribe to the 10,000,000 pages per year current output, the cost per copy for all of the material in microfiche form would be $28,000. Allen Kent has mentioned the figure of 10,000,000 pages for a year's current output of periodical material to be included in this program. It would seem that Dr. Harrer's figure of $40,000 a year should provide some leeway for reinvestment in film.

### Allen Kent
*(as Chairman)*

These cost figures, incidentally, have not taken into account the royalty problem and we'll hear from the publishers tomorrow morning.

Before Dr. Osborn starts I would like to explain how responses will be made to the working papers and particularly to Dr. Warren's proposal. There are four panels representing four different types of library situations. The first panel relates to institutions which have recently completed library buildings, with "recently" being interpreted rather broadly.

The second panel includes those that are committed in regard to new buildings and are in an advanced state of planning or construction.

The third panel represents those that are planning new library buildings but are not yet committed.

*(Here followed a summary of Chapter 3 by Dr. Osborn who provided the transition between the proposed system and the discussion of microform by covering influences exerted by new planning programs on the design of buildings.)*

# PART III

# RESPONSES BY PANELS

# CHAPTER 6

# RECENTLY COMPLETED LIBRARIES

Kenneth S. Allen

Taking Dr. Warren at his word that he wanted some criticism and without in any way rejecting his idea that the Federal government should feel concern and exercise leadership in the availability and dissemination of the scientific and technical information, I remain unconvinced that the creation of a centralized agency of the type proposed is the answer at present. There are substantial questions concerned with the information needs of scientists and engineers, the utility of existing storage and retrieval mechanisms, and the availability of trained or trainable personnel to be resolved before a program such as the one envisioned, with its rather massive outlays, should be pushed forward.

Despite a relatively voluminous literature on the information needs of scientists and technologists, their precise nature remains none too clear—at least none too clear to me. What has been shown is the extremely wide variation in needs from one science to another, and from science in general to technology in general. Where more effective document retrieval might be the answer in one field, information retrieval is needed in another. In some fields of pure science the report literature would be of little moment; in other technical fields, of the greatest importance.

The goal of a unified thesaurus or glossary appears to be rather difficult to attain and perhaps altogether undesirable. It is highly doubtful that such an instrument could serve the varying needs, vocabularies, and contexts of all the sciences and technology. Neither does the suggested process of employing panels of scientists to create these thesauri appear practicable in view of their dedication to other concerns and the extremely detailed nature of such work. This work, it seems to me, does not lend itself to committee action. Committees can set policies; as administrative bodies, they succeed too seldom.

Existing techniques of literature searching by mechanized means have not yet proven themselves. Although much has been learned, much remains to be learned. The problem of balancing precision of need and amount of matter retrieved has not yet been resolved. Commitment on the scale envisaged to techniques neither final in themselves nor necessarily easily compatible, with as yet unthought of future systems, appears unwise.

The problem of securing personnel is a very serious one. The "information scientist" should ideally combine scientific knowledge (how broad?) with library or documental knowledge and skill. People with both scientific skills and information skills are not, I believe, frequently found. It appears, or at least the assumption is frequently made, that it is more practical to teach scientists librarianship than vice versa. However, to get effectively practicing scientists into the literature field will require lures of one kind or another; and it seems likely that these lures must be remuneration during training and after, equal to or beyond that attainable as a scientist. It is not yet apparent to me that at the present instructional facilities equipped and manned to train such scientists can become rapidly available, even with the aid of large-scale institutional subsidies from the government. There has been some action recently that has changed my thinking somewhat on this latter point; however, these negative comments, it must be repeated, refer to the proposal itself, not to the need for governmental concern in the generation and dissemination of scientific and technical information. It is my feeling that governmental efforts would be more effectively expended if they were, for the near future, devoted to monetary support in the following areas:

1. Subsidy to existing nongovernmental bibliographical services to enable them to meet the increases in recorded information.

2. Increased support of governmental information services and specialized centers to plan expansion and correlation of services more adequately.

3. Governmental subsidy to create facilities for teaching "in-

formation science" in conjunction with library schools, including physical facilities, faculty salaries, and other expenses such as equipment, machines, computers, etc.

4. Governmental subsidy in the form of scholarships or fellowships to students of "information science" of number and magnitudes similar to those available to students of physical and biological sciences.

5. Continued and augmented support of researches into the nature of science information needs and informational and documentary storage and retrieval.

6. Dr. Warren's proposal coupled with Mr. Freedman's hardware proposal, I think, overlooks an elementary fact; this is related to the position of the large academic library separated geographically from other academic centers with some heavy demands made upon it in terms of an expanding inter-library loan service. Because the use of microforms is essentially library oriented, I see no way at the moment for the doctor or dentist in the small isolated community who needs a copy of an article in one of the recent journals to obtain it under the system as proposed.

7. The seventh point that I wish to make is that there are some large academic libraries which are located in proximity to private industrial firms with large research organizations. From personal experience I know that such organizations place a heavy demand on nearby library collections. For several reasons, which may be appropriate to my own situation, it seems desirable to continue such relationships. Assuming that it is desirable to continue to serve such organizations, how will the Warren proposal affect our ability to provide such service?

8. The final comment is—and this probably stems from my background as an acquisitions librarian—the plan does not in itself advocate adding any new source materials to the total national stack. Perhaps this is an oversight which can easily be corrected, and I hope that it will be.

Please do not construe the foregoing remarks as lack of interest or a reluctance to participate in any program to make information more readily available. By looking at the proposal in a negative way, I hope only to serve as the devil's advocate and to alert Dr. Warren to some of the problems he faces.

## William N. Locke

It is rather odd to be called someone who has just completed a library, as ours is twelve years old. We expect in ten or fifteen years to have another. In the meantime, we have to remodel or build at least one small one a year. I suspect that is true of everybody, in whatever position he appears on these panels. Frankly, I just don't know of any librarian who isn't planning a library except Vic Schaefer of Notre Dame. His was dedicated a month ago.

## Victor A. Schaefer

Although Notre Dame has just completed its new library and is not planning another, there are a few changes which could be made if we knew in 1958, when we began to plan, what we know today about library automation.

## William N. Locke

All you have to do is take another job somewhere else.

I had a number of comments to Dr. Warren's proposal, but the trouble is I don't like to make them because they are all minor. My major reaction is favorable, in the sense that I feel that it has a great likelihood of being accepted, of becoming a law, though possibly not in this identical form. After reading through the paper and listening to Dr. Warren's presentation, I feel it is a masterful orchestration of goodies for everybody at considerable expense to the taxpayers; but we have suffered long and we shall continue to suffer. As somebody said, "If money isn't spent this way, it will be spent some other way." As Dr. Warren said in starting out, he carefully avoided stepping on anybody's toes. I know that when you can wrap up a package that offends nobody and has something that pleases everybody, it is made. Please accept any further comment I have to make in the light of this general reaction which is thoroughly optimistic.

Most of my criticisms will be rejected because they run right into obviously necessary political considerations without which the package will not be salable. For instance, I think that it would be worth studying whether, with the availability of good communications getting cheaper all the time, it would not be a lot cheaper to set up one central technology library and connect all the different, scattered 100–200 smaller resources that Dr. Warren is talking about by a communications network. I think the area centers are very uneconomical but I can see their political value in the Senate.

I noticed with interest that Boston and New York and all of New England are lumped in one area. This will appeal to those who say too large a proportion of our research funds are in the area of New England. But there is an internal contradiction in the presentation because you will find there the statement that the regional libraries should be located in proportion to the research effort. It is a little shocking to find a regional library in Washington and one for the Northeast—in other words, two to cover the whole area of the East Coast from Virginia to the tip of Maine. All the others are scattered around, some in areas that have very little research effort.

I suspect that one could make a good economic argument for just one center connected by communication links, though one would have to take into account the cost of the communications. This cost is a very substantial factor.

It is so substantial that when we considered about five years ago trying to get a facsimile hookup to transmit between my library and the Lincoln Library which is fifteen miles away over hills, we had to abandon the idea. They have a good library, but they need our larger collections constantly. We looked into this and found it was going to cost $14,000 for a microwave station at each end, $28,000 altogether. It would be a little cheaper to rent coaxial cable, but it was still far cheaper to copy the article on a copying machine and put it on the shuttle bus, which goes every hour. To be sure, instead of getting it in three minutes, it takes three hours, but the cost is negligible.

In any regional or national system of distribution we should try to figure out the most economical way. Our telegraph and telephone people have franchises which mean that we have to pay commercial rates, even with communications satellites. Some new method of communication may come along but in the meantime economics will determine whether we use a very inexpensive communication network, the U. S. Mail or expensive wire or radio links.

I am very much disturbed by one of the definitions in the proposal. I wish Dr. Warren, before it goes further, would change his definition of "published scientific literature." He defines this as journal literature. The published literature has always included and will continue to include books and monographs. It may or may not include technical reports, which Dr. Warren specifically omits from his proposal. It is a mistake to define "published literature" as journal literature because it can't help but to confuse a lot of people.

## Stafford L. Warren

I didn't mean to. I agree that the journals are only a part of the open literature.

## William N. Locke

I wish you would look at it again. I am delighted to have you control the bibliography of journal articles, but the fact is that, in spite of the bad time lag, we have pretty good control there. On the other hand, we don't have control of report literature. If you are going to do a real job for science and technology, you ought to think bigger and include journals, reports, and books. You don't have a library of science and technology unless you do. What you propose is only a library of journal articles. This is a fraction, an important fraction, but you will find if you go around and ask a few engineers, that they feel that report literature is more important than journal literature. Anyway it seems to me you cannot honestly call this a library of science and technology if you are only servicing the journal literature.

I like very much your idea of standardized terminology. It is necessary—it is essential that we have this. Somehow stronger teeth need to be put into the bill to bring about coordination between the agencies who will be feeding information into your system. You say that the presence of the advisory committee representing the various agencies will bring this about. I am afraid I have to question this, having been on advisory committees in Washington and having seen what happens. Take, for example, the Department of Defense. For fifteen years there have been directives that all research organizations under the Department of Defense are required to submit a copy of all reports to DDC or to ASTIA. They don't. It's been estimated that 30 percent of the reports produced by defense-sponsored projects never get into the system. This is within one department. What chance do you think there is that directives agreed to or listened to by representatives of a dozen government agencies around a table will really get implemented? A realistic view would indicate that we have got to have a much stronger approach—you did mention in your oral presentation that you hope the President would urge cooperation on the professional societies. They are more amenable, but government agencies, on the basis of my experience, have enormous inertia. This is a tough question. I don't believe you have really faced up to the difficulty of getting cooperation along the lines of standardization of the computer languages and on the matter of standardization of terminology.

While it is very nice to add to the proposal a little nest egg for machine-translation research, frankly, we don't need it. This is a field I have been in since the beginning, and the National Science Foundation has been more than generous. I think that you will find that people in the field around the country will agree with me. It would be out and out waste to put more money into it.

Another point on English. The English teachers and professors in the country may take your money, but they are not going to be interested in the work you have in mind. Linguists are interested but most English teachers are not. They are interested in literature, so I would suggest that they are the wrong recipients for the grant that you propose to give for the investigation of language. Moreover, linguistics research is already well financed by the National Science Foundation.

Now I will turn to Mr. Freedman's paper. I wish that we had here in the room a representative of Bell & Howell's film division because it would be most interesting to hear what he would have to say in response to various points. One would almost think Bell & Howell is not in the business of selling microfilm— I'd like to have heard the dialogue but I am not going to be able to carry it on for lack of information. Still, I would like to mention a few aspects of microfiche which Mr. Freedman didn't mention. One thing, for instance, is rather serious. It is that, in spite of the fact that government agencies have arrived at some mechanical standards for microfiche, they have not arrived at any quality standards. There are quality standards for microfilm which insured, or did until the measles broke out, that we get reliable film. I am sorry to say that the government standards as agreed upon have the very unfortunate disadvantage that the microfiche run 12 images by 5, which means you have to use two digits to identify location in the 12 columns and one digit for the 5. It would have been better from the point of view of the future if we had a standard where we could specify by a single digit in each dimension, 9 by 9, for instance. In any mechanized system this would save a lot of money. It may be too late to do anything about this but it is not too late to get quality standards set up for microfiche.

I have to disagree with Mr. Freedman on microfiche readers. I don't think there is a decent one on the market. His company is working on one and I hope it will be better. It is my understanding that Mr. Freedman is not planning to provide negatives at the moment. We need negatives so that we can give our customers positives. The customers, who hate microimages anyway, hate negatives even more. Reading white on black is too hard on the eye whether it be film or fiche.

Mr. Freedman also made the comment that the fiche is less complicated than the film. This is true if you are searching manually but not if you are searching by machine. If you have ever seen Eastman's Minicard and seen the mechanical complication of handling those chips of film, then you can imagine what sort of machinery would be necessary to sort these microfiches by machine, transport them, and blow them up. We are talking about very complicated machinery. We have to have not only large-scale reproduction, but also some way of sorting these microfiches mechanically. If you take the 15 linear feet of shelving and put all those boxes containing all those journals on those shelves, then consider how many people are going to want access at the same time to those boxes. You are going to have the worst traffic jam you ever saw; you are going to have 30, 40, 50 people, all of whom are going to want access to some part of those 15 linear feet at the same time. This is why we must have mechanical sorting as well as rapid printing. Compactness may actually cost more in money and inconvenience than storing the original documents.

My last two points refer to Dr. Osborn's presentation. First, as to the Grand Valley experiment, I would suggest that what they are trying to do is go back to the situation in which a number of underdeveloped countries find themselves today. The way they are proposing to teach is pretty much the way schools are taught in India and Africa: there are no books and they are trying awfully hard to get them. It seems the height of absurdity to turn back the clocks to medieval times and do without books when we have books. It is incredible to me that anybody would put up money for such a ridiculous experiment.

Second, I agree again with Dr. Osborn. Both earlier speakers emphasized the "chaos" in the libraries of the world today. I haven't seen it, and I don't believe it. Everybody is saying that soon we'll slowly smother to death under mountains of paper. It isn't here yet. As far as I can see, the libraries are working and people are finding the information they want to find. Research goes on pretty well. I don't think the chaos that has been described is even imminent, but I am perfectly willing to prepare for the future—prepare for the day when chaos would come if we didn't get going. That is why I am pleased to hear Dr. Warren's and Mr. Freedman's suggestions to possible solutions.

## John H. Moriarty

I took seriously this idea that I was in a recently completed library and I interpreted my concern to be the effect on library buildings. And so I will talk very largely to that idea rather than in any way criticize Dr. Warren's proposal. As a matter of fact, though, I will agree—I will accept his proposal. You may be sorry later how I'll accept it. If I accept Dr. Warren's proposal, however, we are going to have a remarkable institutional problem. I think this proposal concerns many things besides universities, and I hope nobody will think that I believe it only involves universities. It certainly does not. But insofar as it involves universities, it involves me; and, therefore, egocentrically I am determined that our library will adjust to it, because I am determined that there are not to be two systems of information on my campus under two different administrations. There will be one system of information under one group of professionally minded people. Now, if this means throwing the librarians out, I suspect the librarians will have to be thrown out.

The bankers of the United States in 1935 or so had shown that they were inadequate for the needs of this country's financial growth and most of the old timers were kicked out, and a whole new breed of bankers had to be introduced in order to forward this economy of ours; and I very much suspect that a whole new breed of information officers will have to be introduced to forward this country's information problems, if librarians don't rise to the occasion. I think there is no reason why they shouldn't rise to it. The reason I believe in unitary systems of information control, if you will, on a campus, is based on the analogy that Dr. Warren used—an analogy of the library's being the heart of the university. I am sick of that, and so are all the librarians. I would prefer it to be called the nervous system of the institution; and I think you can only have one nervous system. If you get signals of two kinds floating around the campus, you are likely to have real chaos not merely with material but with people; so I feel the call here not for being antagonistic to Dr. Warren or being antagonistic to librarians, but rather the call for an internal activity in the library of a program of operations research. We need not accept that we need a computer; we need to know what we need to do, where the computer fits in and where traditional systems fit in. Or is that what we should use—in other words, I don't believe in taking the computer, except as one more ancillary operation, just as over the years we have taken in the journal and taken in the other new media. I feel that the two kinds of adjustments have necessarily to be made. I think Dr. Warren very carefully discussed the problem or repeatedly came back to the problem of the responsibility of the professional groups such as medicine for their own information opportunities both by their internal skills in discovering things and then in their care that they themselves retrieved things. This has always been the function of the scholar and you, Dr. Warren, bring it out. And another very nice point to it—that the scholar not only finds what he is looking for but he finds what he should have been looking for; which, I think, can only come to the scholar who takes on himself the responsibility for finding his information. I think in a way when people say that the engineer is a kind of man who depends on the librarian, whereas a scientist insists on taking care of himself in the library (and Saul Herner and others have developed this idea while studying the habits of these researchers). I think they are simply pointing at the immaturity, in a way, of the engineering profession's members, still not accepting this responsibility for their own service. Now this does not mean though that librarians aren't responsible also for the system; not the service, if you will, but for the system and to see that the system, particularly for the whole institution, coordinates. It will be a sorry day when the chemist doesn't think to order me around; it will be a sorry day when I don't tell him he's talking nonsense on occasion. This is the way all important powerful groups handle each other in a society, not by having one tell the other you can do this and you can't do that. So I insist, when asking the professions to be self responsible, that they not at the same time think that I am stupid. I know better, and I have fought years for what I have. However, I am very optimistic about this.

I have had, as part of my building experience, the responsibility for planning a building in 1953 and 1954 and putting into it the audio-visual activities of a campus of 20,000 people; and all I had was an idea or a set of ideas. All my ideas have been changed, but the building has stood up amazingly I find because of the talent of the users. I find that the students were not trying to fool the library staff into waiting on them. The students are miraculous self-users of the services and have remarkable ways of taking care of themselves. I find that if I depend on them to self-serve themselves, they rise to the occasion all the time. I was told by the audio-visual people around the country that you couldn't trust a student with a projector and a film. We have to teach 500-600 freshmen, and only that number out of 3,000 each year, how to thread a film; and after one or at the most two lessons, they pick up a film from our loan desks exactly as they pick up a book. They go and serve themselves on a projector and see what they are supposed to see individually and personally and then return the film to us all wrapped up. They do the same things with tapes. There is no problem here. On the other hand, I will admit that I have seen librarians who that insisted upon threading the projector for the student, who insisted upon threading the tape, who would not allow the student to do these things. I don't know what they are going to do when we have these eight-millimeter shorts for individual viewing by students. They are going to have chaos. They are going to come to an impasse, but this is because these librarians aren't giving the materials to the students and letting these people, brilliant young people, in almost every instance, take care of themselves.

I have been told that professors hate microfilm. A year ago on May 1, on Alumni Day, Saturday morning, I was patrolling the library—as I do—and I came across the typical yellow and black box that the *New York Times* on microfilm reels is kept in at my institution. There it was on the floor opened up and empty; and, of course, being the old snooper that I am, I looked at that and then I looked around, and I saw another box on the floor (this one fortunately had the film wrapped up pretty well but not exactly). Well, I looked farther afield and I was terrified at what I might be running into. I noticed an open stack window, so I looked out. There among the rhododendrons two floors down was this high pile of film. I went down and retrieved my film, and came back through the library. Then I got it onto the microfilm reader and verified. We had our piece alright, but it turned out when I put this second box back that a third box was wholly missing. Well, I really started scouring the place then from fear of such a loss (and I got quite breathless). Almost at once I was called to the telephone by one of the vice presidents who wanted some information, and he said, "What are you puffing for?" and I said, "You and your students!" He said, "What do you mean?" I said, "Why, I just got this microfilm out of the mud outside the building." He said, "What do you mean? Where?" I told him, and he said, "Is that what I saw last night?" And I said, "What did you see last night?" "I was walking with some of the fellows across campus behind the library when we saw three streamers of microfilm hanging out of the back stack window, and a girl who was going by went over and touched it and she said it was damp; so I thought you were just drying film." I said, "No, I wasn't." Well, we ordered a replacement for the missing half month of the *New York Times*, but before we got the replacement we found the box behind the books on a shelf in the stacks—one of the pages discovered it; and so our film file is now complete.

But the point of my story is that the students use these things just that casually. There is no resistance among them at all; and if the older professors don't, well they will leave soon enough. So, I feel, Mr. Freedman, that whatever your material is, if we need it we'll use it; and we'll use all pieces of it.

I find the English Department perfectly willing to read three centuries of English drama on micro-opaque sheets. They think nothing of it. The early American imprints are used constantly. There is no great resistance to these. And so I am quite optimistic on all this material.

I realize I live among a group of scientists and engineers largely, and although we have increasing change, our students are casual about this. For example, the slide rule, once the engineer's trademark, is gone. What you see now is the student trotting around the campus with these computer printout sheets under his arm and his little pack of cards folded in the middle. He sits and types out his program onto his cards; and this is just the most ordinary thing in the world to him. Actually, I can remember when the faculty was not going to have the students use the computer. Well, the students took care of this: every student problem is an unconventional problem now.

There are no more trivial problems in our engineering course—all problems are computer problems.

Now about Dr. Osborn's paper. I told Dr. Osborn that I thought, to borrow the terms from the mathematician, that his paper was "elegant." It seems to me he has woven into it every concern that we people, as librarians, are subject to; and this is a very, very important thing—that all of these concerns be woven in. I am going to take some of Mr. Berthel's thunder away from him to illustrate the institutional complexity of the library. He sent me a report on their operations research study, which was a wonderfully generous thing to do, and I read it, and in reading it I found the big hole in his study. He had made 3,000 observations on readers (this is right, about 3,000), and, of course, this seemed like a good sample—any behavioral scientist would have said 3,000 was a good sample. But that scientist wasn't studying library behaviors, because what the Johns Hopkins group found when they studied this behavior activity of people in libraries was that it was so mixed up that they couldn't get any decent statistical categorization out of it.

A professor would come in for some data. He would also borrow a book for his wife and read the *New York Times* and something else and go home, and this is what investigators had to analyze. By the time they tried to sort out how many pure activities of one kind or another they had, no one activity had a statistically reliable sample. What you would have to have is 15,000 or 20,000 case studies to get something statistically reliable for this library behavior. This is why, Dr. Warren, I dare to welcome you as just one more problem. We librarians will take care of you and your wife and the high school students from your family and the other faculty families, and now this new filmed science hoard, and this is what we will have to do. This is our problem as a complex institution. I don't think this is your problem in furnishing a national service, you see. We'll have to adapt to you and your integration into our services.

Now, as to the other points that Dr. Osborn brought out, I have a suggestion. If I were specifying for a university about its library building for any of the sciences, I would specify that the conduit be sewer-pipe size. I mean nothing less will do. Actually if there isn't some hole in every 10 square feet of wall or floor around the library building it is inadequately wired for the future.

None of us is ready for the problems that are about to fall

in on our heads, and those problems go right on. There is no question about it. At one moment we are assailed about a very special retrieval problem for which we have to get a junior investigator all groomed and send him down to Washington to the DOD's DDC to spend a week pulling out the "poop." The next moment a faculty wife comes into the office, and she's sure she's got the *Ulster County Gazette* for April, 1800. I have to prove to her by so many rules and lines that "Madam, you don't have the original. This is not worth $50,000." So, if I were speaking from the point of view of building, I would say that we have to make space for all of these things and I am sure that in another 10 years if we make mistakes of planning too timidly it will be even wilder.

### Stafford L. Warren

I think there is no disagreement with Dr. Locke about the importance of Departments of English. It just depends on the organization of the campus. Some universities are more familiar with the name—Linguistic Department. It is word form and composition, so it doesn't matter where the department is located—it is the same people we're talking about.

### William N. Locke

Maybe anthropology, maybe linguistics.

### Stafford L. Warren

Yes, I agree. I don't believe that there is enough money being spent on machine translation. I'd like to see more or less perfect machines come out as soon as possible.

### William N. Locke

I could talk on the subject, but I don't think it is the time. I'll talk about it later with you.

### Stafford L. Warren

Is it near?

### William N. Locke

It depends on just what you mean. Now you can grind out a quick translation, but it won't be a good translation. The trouble is the higher you want to go in quality, the more money you have got to put into it and the fewer people can work it.

## Stafford L. Warren

The higher you go, you ought to be able to read it yourself. The machine can't yet get it finished perfectly.

## William N. Locke

That's the point. You can get 95 percent of the words translated, but are you satisfied with that? The chances are you are not. The other 5 percent would convey the information you wanted. You have got to go to 98 or 99 percent and even then is it enough, or does the output have to be edited by someone who can read the language? There have been millions of words translated by CIA and other organizations who are just grinding them out but they hardly are usable unless you know the language; that is, unless you want to take the chance of being radically wrong. The best you can say is that the poor translation is good enough to see if this paper ought to be translated professionally. That is already a step forward.

## Stafford L. Warren

Now as to the open literature. I was only distinguishing between the published scientific journals and the classified files and government reports. Of course, I agree that the government reports are very important elements in all of this. But after looking at a lot of committee reports on the subject and talking with the people in the Department of Commerce and elsewhere, I felt that it would complicate the situation to bring in these parcels at this time. If Commerce and others dealing with this report literature would use the same standards and glossaries so that they become compatible with the journal literature, then at that time these reports could be absorbed by the system or they could be hooked in as a special group that would be available to anyone who wanted them.

## William N. Locke

What you are saying then is if Commerce wants the reports you are not going to take them away; but if Commerce doesn't want them, you're willing to take them?

## Stafford L. Warren

The Department of Commerce already has them and should continue to serve their public.

William N. Locke

They have got a new man who is good, and maybe they'll do better.

Stafford L. Warren

The representative from the Department of Commerce is a member of the Operating Advisory Committee so we hope that we will gain on both sides.

The centers were extensively discussed over almost a whole year. They have several problems. The one you mention—the communication from one installation to another—could be by wire or post or any other convenient method. By having many centers you cut down on the supposed cost of these communications, particularly if you can devise a network where most of the centers are in areas of density of the users.

William N. Locke

Each center will cost you how many dollars?

Stafford L. Warren

It depends whether it is on a primary, secondary or tertiary level.

William N. Locke

I am talking about primary. You could go directly from one primary to a secondary center. You could save a good many millions of dollars that you would need to build other centers.

Stafford L. Warren

Not very much actually, because these centers in terms of libraries aren't very costly. I am talking in the neighborhood of seven or eight million dollars including the education, research, and development, and conference facilities in the building.

William N. Locke

Seven or eight millions times 7, including Washington.

Stafford L. Warren

For the secondary centers.

## William N. Locke

I do not question the utility of secondary centers at all, but whether you need this constellation of primary centers which is going to cost 50 million dollars to build. It's a cost consideration.

## Stafford L. Warren

This could be determined by studying the needs of the system when these councils and committees are set up. The allocation of funds for construction doesn't come until the third, fourth, fifth, or sixth years.

## William N. Locke

But politically this idea of a group of centers is a better sales mechanism than one center.

## Stafford L. Warren

Yes, but I weigh that rather low in my priority. It is the long distance cost. On the other hand, you may have the rolls of tape or microfilm duplicated and mail them. You haven't lost anything but a day or so. The best method won't come out until after a year or so of study and trial. It is a moot question, and it has to be studied; so I don't think I would disagree very violently. Would you accept the proposal that there should be some kind of organization that could study this, make some recommendations as to a director and a system which is capable of allotting sufficient funds to do the work. Such an organization does not exist today. It would have to be created, and it would take legislation to do it. That would be my reply to Dr. Allen's six or seven stipulations, because there is a mechanism set up in the proposal for an advisory council and study section, advising and recommending on all of the requirements for the new system—the education, the research and R&D pilot programs, the paying for the conferences, even for the backlog of publications. If it seems necessary to catch up the blacklog in journals which are one and a half to two years behind, I would make the subsidy directly to bring them up to date. The construction of these facilities would have to go through application and approval with a priority set by council, project site visits— all of this machinery that the NIH agency operates so successfully and no other agency has. It seems to me this would be a very good feature. It's democratic and representative of the appropriate professions. The contractual arrangement with universities to design and operate these programs at the secondary level in conjunction with their training and research programs is another important feature. It should also occur at the primary level where this is feasible. I think that it is practical for the government to do this. I think there is no other way of doing it if we are to stimulate and enlist the best minds in this new field.

If nothing more transpires right now, I think this net will grow up like Topsy through the National Medical Library, National Institutes of Health, and other government agencies piecemeal. The universities that can get some kind of grant money or even their own money will support slowly but inevitably their library educational programs in developing these new people. I hope that nothing disturbs the relationship of the librarian except that he has got to do as you say—move over and bring this new group in and adjust to it. The computer at first is just a different kind of catalog for citations and bibliography and later abstracts and other things included in the store. I don't know about how soon the facsimile can be put into the computer tape system. It may be microfiche or something else that will come along as the art develops. As long as your building is flexible and your own people are flexible and you have graduate students coming up, you will adjust.

### Samuel Freedman

I want to respond to Mr. Locke. In one section he said that he wished there were a representative of Bell & Howell in his audience and there is.

### William N. Locke

Are you he?

### Samuel Freedman

I am he.

I agree with you that quality standards are needed. There are quality standards in certain areas, particularly in work done for the Department of Defense. It would not be easy, probably impossible, to set up standards to cover all microfilming problems.

I think a great deal depends on the organization and the technicians who are actually doing the work.

I am glad you brought up the matter of the so-called "J" spots.

As most of you probably know, microscopic blemishes have been found on some microfilm which has been stored for a period of two to twenty years. I do not minimize the findings as a potential source of danger to archival records which have been placed on film. A great deal of effort, time and money are being directed to this problem and progress is being made. I believe it is fair to say, however, that the "J" spot problem has been blown up out of proportion due to the publicity disseminated by persons and organizations not familiar completely with the technical aspects of the problem. In some cases brief and "out of context" publicity has raised a great deal of unwarranted alarm. Keep in mind that the incidence of spots is low. Loss of information on microfilm caused by "J" spots has been rare. Work is going on by responsible organizations and persons knowledgeable in this field. Keep in mind that other mediums for preserving permanent records have been menaced by hazards of various types in the past. Paper and ink, on which most of the world's permanent records have been recorded for hundreds of years have raised some problems. There has been improvement in this area and we are certain that the "J" spot problem will be resolved satisfactorily. For those wishing to learn more about film blemishes we recommend Handbook 96 entitled *Inspection of Processed Photographic Record Films for Aging Blemishes* which has been produced by the National Bureau of Standards and is available from the U. S. Government Printing Office for 25 cents. We recommend also an article entitled "Microscopic Spots and Processed Microfilm" which appeared in the publication *Photographic Science and Engineering*, Volume 7, Number 5, September-October 1963, beginning with page 253. [Note: Since this talk was given, the *National Micro-News,* official journal of the National Microfilm Association, devoted practically an entire issue —No. 70, June 1964—to this subject and it is highly recommended reading for those wishing to be informed.] Mr. Locke stated that there is a great deal of room for improvement in reading machines for use with microfiche. I can only agree with this statement and would like to assure this group that there is development along this line. If the market for microfiche develops as I believe it will, the demand will surely be filled.

Dr. Locke asked whether negative microfiche copies could be provided as well as positives. This is no problem. It costs no more to produce negatives than to produce positives, but I would like to give a little further background on this question. It is my personal belief that it is better in many cases from the viewing standpoint to work with a positive image. Where there are illustrations it is much better to view the positive image than a negative. Most people are more accustomed to reading copy in positive form than in negative and the light output of a reader need not be as great in viewing positive film as it should be in reading negative. Over the life of most viewers on the market today the light output decreases progressively unless excellent maintenance is adhered to. There are certain reasons, in my opinion, for the use of negative film. "Reader-printer" equipment presently on the market produces positive hard copy best from a negative film image. Reader-printers which use silver paper reverse the image. That is, they produce a positive print from a negative image and a negative print from a positive image. One of the most popular "reader-printers" on the market today produces much better prints from a negative film than from a positive. Another factor to be considered is that if you reproduce film copies using diazo films you get a negative copy from a negative. In other words, diazo does not reverse. I have heard people say that reading from negative film on a reader screen is easier on the eyes. I have never found this to be true and, in fact, I prefer to read positive film and I suppose I have viewed as much microfilm on reader screens as most people. It is a matter of preference and mechanics and, as I said, either positive or negative prints are available.

Dr. Locke has raised another interesting question as to the possibility of loss or misfiling of individual microfiche. I believe that there is a possibility of loss or misfiling with the unitized file, this possibility being greater than it would be with roll mocrofilm. There are certain advantages in using a unitized file and I believe these advantages are greater than the disadvantages. This is not a new question since the same question has been with us with conventional records which are kept on paper. Record keeping on paper evolved from the scroll to the bound book to the loose leaf book and to the vertical card file. I believe the same questions were raised with paper records. Yet, the use of the vertical card file is universal. Many important records are maintained in this fashion and, in fact, the punch card files are maintained in this manner.

I believe that the microfiche offers a number of advantages that override the disadvantages for the National Science Library System.

1. Microfiche lends itself to quick and economical card to card reproduction. If I understand the requirements of the National Science Library System properly, there will be a demand for individual articles. It is much easier and more economical to use microfiche for this purpose than it is to use roll film. At least this is true at the present time and I believe it will continue to be true. (Note: Replacement cards, if needed, are quickly and inexpensively available by this method.)
2. Microfiche will make possible the development of good, low-cost reading equipment.
3. The finding speed of the vertical card system is superior to the roll for this application.

Perhaps this statement is oversimplified and I am sure a great deal more discussion could be had on this subject, but I believe that microfiche is the best medium for the periodicals to be included in the National Science Library System.

I believe it would be possible to mechanize the retrieval of microfiche provided money was available for research and development. I would like to point out, however, that a good vertical file, properly guided and housed, offers excellent finding and filing speed.

## William N. Locke

The reasons I want negatives is because we don't want our customers to use the file copies of films. You sell to us; we want to make the positive to put it in readers. In other words, I am not disagreeing that people want positives. They want both positive film and positive prints; but the best way for us to give them positives without having to go through a couple of generations is for you to sell us negatives with a high reduction. Have you read "The Future of Research Library"? In it Clapp says the future of research libraries lies in reduction of 100 or 200 diameters, that we have got to stop playing around with small reduction; we have got to go into large reduction and then blow up to full size in the next step.

## Andrew D. Osborn

If there is any risk that there might be two streams of information in a university, it is extremely important for the university library to set to work and to adapt and make sure that there is a single stream. This is one of the most difficult things we face, and it is extremely important that we develop a common philosophy; otherwise we run the risk of having the library on one side and information scientists on the other. Just make sure that we do have a single line of communication for information, for both bibliographical control and textual control. I see the great challenge at the present time: The bringing together of these two streams so each with its knowledge, each with its skills, each with its insights, will help and strengthen the other. I think he put his finger on a very critical matter in the whole picture.

## Allen Kent

Before going on to the next panel, there is one question I'd like to direct to Ken Allen since he took the negative position in this matter: Should a national science library system be successful in getting started, how would you react to it with regard to wanting service? Would you still say "no"?

## Kenneth S. Allen

We'll be part of it. I only tried to point out some things that need some further study. People read in a lot of ways and in a lot of places—and anything which will increase this intellectual intake—my library will be for 100 percent.

# CHAPTER 7

# LIBRARIES COMMITTED BY
# ACTIVE PLANNING OR CONSTRUCTION

Allen Kent
*(as Chairman)*

The next panel is represented by the four men who presumably have libraries in active planning or active construction. I know one of the panelists finished his library between the time of our invitation and his arrival at this meeting. But we ask if he will act as if he is still not completely finished, since this would be nice for the purposes of panel discussion. The panel members are John H. Berthel of Johns Hopkins University, Edward M. Heiliger of Florida Atlantic University, Victor A. Schaefer of Notre Dame, and George Mallinson of Western Michigan University.

John H. Berthel

There is a refreshing simplicity in the proposal submitted by Dr. Warren and his associates, and this simplicity is not the least of the proposal's attractions.

It is obvious that scientists, librarians and information specialists have become increasingly aware of the problems of bibliographical control posed by the exponential growth of scientific literature.

In the years following World War II it is unusual to find an agenda for a meeting of any of these professional groups that does not contain some reference to these problems.

It is also obvious that more and more people are excited by

119

the potential of the new machinery, looking upon it as the most useful tool yet devised, for providing a resolution of these problems.

It is at this point, however, that the word "obvious" begins to disappear from the discussion. Up to this time in our history there have been many theories expressed concerning the use to be made of the new machinery but relatively little specific agreement among the protagonists as to the best use to be made of it.

One example of this diversity of opinion is found in the fact that, during the past fifteen years, a new profession has emerged in this field, the documentalist or information specialist. This group, trained in the use of the new machinery, is sometimes of the opinion that the librarian is so closely wedded to traditional methods that he must be by-passed, if not ignored, if full advantage is to be taken of the new machinery's potential.

It is true that some librarians have looked askance at the computer and viewed it as somehow being a threat to humanistic scholarship.

In each group those holding these extreme views are in the minority and their number declines daily as knowledge concerning the new machinery grows.

There have been other and more practical reasons for the relatively slow acceptance of the new machinery for library purposes by some librarians. Among these have been the high costs of acquiring and operating the computers, and the fact that, until quite recently, the machines were designed for use in industry and government and for solving problems not necessarily directly related to the bibliographical control problems faced by libraries.

The size and nature of the bibliographical control problem and its importance to the scientific research effort of this country is more clearly understood, and this understanding has led to the development and manufacture of computers readily adapted to this new use.

As a result of these and other recent developments, Dr. Warren's report is extraordinarily timely.

One might quarrel with the proposal that attention first be focused on scientific journals. A reasonable degree of bibliographical control exists in this area. Although certainly not under perfect bibliographical control, this literature is definitely not in a chaotic state. Indices, abstracting services, and other bibliographic aids provide useful guides to the contents of scientific journals.

Under much poorer control, at the moment, is the technical and scientific report literature. The practicing librarian would be pleased if this material could quickly be brought under bibliographical control comparable to that already provided for journal literature.

This is not intended as a serious criticism of Dr. Warren's proposal, for he does not ignore the importance of tackling the problem posed by the report literature.

The "refreshing simplicity" of Dr. Warren's proposal is that he picks, for immediate attention, an area of scientific literature that could, with relative ease, be programmed for, and stored in, the computer's memory. He sets up an initial goal that is comprehensible to anyone with even an educated layman's knowledge of the new machinery's capabilities.

It also seems reasonable to assume, along with Dr. Warren, that the size and complexity of the total task ahead of us is of such a magnitude that it will require Federal participation and support. Hence, the idea of a national science information center and a number of regional subcenters, makes great good sense.

On the other hand, Dr. Warren's assumption that "MEDLARS be adopted as the physical and administrative starting point for the National Library of Science System and that it be designated as the Washington Center," is one that can, at least, be questioned.

It is on this point that further discussion and deliberation would probably prove to be  definitely worthwhile. MEDLARS may or may not be the most likely candidate but it may be that an equally likely candidate, to name merely one, is the Library of Congress, which over the years has built up a fine tradition of library service to the nation in a wide variety of subject fields.

This final note of caution is seriously submitted but is not intended to detract from the thoughtful and valuable contribution of Dr. Warren and his associates.

Allen Kent
(as Chairman)

You have had an opportunity of starting with a clean slate, Mr. Heiliger.

Edward M. Heiliger

I like Dr. Warren's plan very much but I am tied in my thinking to the Library of Congress. I was on the Advisory Committee for the automation study of the Library of Congress. During my work on that Committee, I pushed for planning that would eventually enable us to order our own printed catalog from the Library of Congress, instead of our LC cards. This catalog would, of course, cover the social sciences and humanities as well as the sciences. At Florida Atlantic University we will be doing this for ours when we open for classes in September of this year.

I would like to tell you about our computer-based system so that you can see the potential of a relationship with a well-developed national system.

All library records will be stored on computer tape. The computer to be used will be an IBM 1460. We have had to develop ways of putting these records onto computer tape so that the computer could print out a variety of "control documents" in such a way that they would be suitable for their various purposes. Among these "control documents" are : the catalog, a daily circulation list, a thrice-weekly current serials list (short title), an annual serials holdings list, and a processing information list. Other printouts include overdue notices, SDI notices, statistical information, book orders, budget information, bibliographies, and special circulation lists (including lists in circulation arranged by ID number).

To provide for the cataloging input and output, we have developed a coding system and a special computer chain which gives a more refined printout with upper and lower case and all of the diacritical marks needed for the Western languages. A coding system has been developed for serials input. Circulation input will be prepared by the IBM 357 data collection system.

In coding cataloging copy for the computer, we find that non-academic personnel can do the coding at a rate of about 75 titles per day. Key-punch operators can average somewhat more than this, but they are hampered by a need for using a special keyboard which we have designed. Authority files are also being put onto tape, and during the initial stages of the creation of the computer catalog this is a large work factor. Proofreading is done on copy produced daily by the computer. This enables the catalog department to catch mistakes being made. The computer output which comes in 17 $\times$ 22-inch sheets, is being reduced 45 percent to make the catalog page 8½ $\times$ 11 inches. There are three columns on each page with an average number of entries of about 40. There will be 150 copies of the catalog produced.

These will be distributed throughout the campus and throughout the library. Monthly supplements will be cumulative up to three months. A new edition of the catalog will be printed out. There will be an author, a subject, and a title catalog. There will be an occasional printout of the shelf list, but a card shelf list will be maintained in the early stages. Parts of the catalog can be loaned out. A central catalog location has been planned. This will look like the out-of-town telephone directory center at O'Hare Airport. It will be a circular counter with copies of the catalog that can be turned down, used and flipped back up into place. There will be no card catalog, which will eliminate all filing of cards and revision of filing. Errors in the catalog can be corrected much more easily. Although the printout will not show as much information as the LC card shows, there will actually be more cataloging information available. This additional cataloging information will be stored on computer tape and will be available for literature searches and bibliographical printout.

For circulation work, the IBM 357 data collection system is going to be tied in with the Registrar and Business Office System also, and will enable the computer to send out overdue notices and to print out the daily circulation list and other circulation information. Fines will be eliminated but the student will be charged for the computer-produced overdue notices. The 357 system will eliminate all filing of cards, and all slipping of books. The books returned to the shelf will be speeded up and the number of errors in circulation work will be greatly reduced. The system is now almost a self-charging system and a few changes in the machinery will make it possible for it to become completely self-charging.

The serials input has to be prepared only once for each serials title. Thereafter, the computer produces a check-in card for each issue of each journal and inserting one of these cards into the system takes the place of posting in a written record. The computer recognizes nonarrival of a journal and writes a letter to the supplier asking for an investigation. The computer prints out lists of journals by subjects, serials orders, and thrice-weekly current serials lists, and an annual serials holdings list. The current serials list indicates whether or not a journal has arrived, and if it has not arrived, when it is expected. Binding lists of books and journals are also printed out.

Several colleges and universities in the southeast Florida area have indicated interest in having their records stored on our tapes and receiving their own catalog and serials printout from us on a contract basis. There has also been talk of eventually having a tape center for all of the State universities in Florida. Beyond this, of course, is regional and national cooperation of the same sort.

## Frazer G. Poole

Members of this panel were selected to represent libraries in the planning or construction phase, for which funds have already been appropriated. Actually, the library I represent, the University of Illinois, Chicago Undergraduate Division, is engaged in a three-phase building program of which only the first unit has been planned or funded. We are thus in a favorable position to take advantage of the results of this conference on "Library Planning for Automation."

Before reacting to the papers I should like to make a few comments about the unit of the building now under construction and about our planning for future units. The basic planning for this first phase, which was carried on under the direction of my predecessor, Edward Heiliger and his staff, envisioned a building with such a degree of flexibility that it could be adapted to any foreseeable development in automation.

A few years ago, as many of you know, Mr. Heiliger and his staff initiated a long-range investigation into the automation of library procedures. In the expectation that a computerized library system would prove feasible, space for a data processing department was included in the first unit of the library. Initially, the library will use computer facilities in the campus computer center. Later, it is expected that the Office of Instructional Resources, which occupies space in the library building, will acquire a computer for research in programmed learning. If so, it is likely that the library can arrange to use this computer.

The final building will contain approximately 1,000 electronic carrells which will serve not only for traditional methods of study, but which will also make it possible for students to view televised lectures on a closed circuit system, to listen to a variety of recorded programs, and to take advantage of the computer-based programmed instruction methods developed by the Office of Instructional Resources.

With the thought that future developments may make it possible to query the memory store of a computer in the Library of Congress or elsewhere, three "console rooms" are being provided adjacent to the library's Reference Department. Initially these will be used as staff offices, but all electrical conduit required for console hook-up will be installed when the building is constructed.

As for my reactions to the papers—it seems to me that Dr. Warren has developed a plan for collecting and disseminating the journal literature of the sciences which would certainly make it possible for libraries to serve the scientific community far more efficiently than we do now. Given adequate funds, the scheme should be possible of accomplishment much as Dr. Warren has outlined it. To relate his proposal to the title of this conference— the efficient administration of such a plan should present no problems for a library planned with normal flexibility.

As regards the choice of medium for the storage of the tremendous quantities of information involved, I strongly second the recommendation for microfiche. The advantages of this form of microtext in easier, more economical reproduction, and in the availability of better reading equipment (as contrasted with the hardware available for reading micro-opaques) are decisive, it seems to me.

Should the plan be put into operation, I would like to emphasize the importance of selecting an acceptable standard for both size and format. Several agencies are now considering the problem of standards for microfiche and, hopefully, firm recommendations in these matters will be available before long.

Despite my generally favorable reaction to the Warren proposal, there are a few points about it that raise questions in my mind. One of these is the matter of cost. I wish this could be reduced to a point at which the scheme might be a little more saleable. Possibly it would be worthwhile to reexamine the proposal with a view to reducing the cost even if this requires some reduction in the scope of the program.

Related to the above is the possible effect of the Warren proposal on the future of the Library of Congress Automation Project. Earlier in this meeting, it was suggested that if the reaction of this group (and others to whom the proposal may be submitted) was favorable, that the Congress, through the Executive branch of the government, might be asked for funds with which to inaugurate the program. While I have no idea as to the action now being taken by the Library of Congress as a result of the report submitted by Gilbert King and his survey team last December, it seems reasonable to assume that in the near future, the Congress may be asked to provide funds for the L.C. program. Of the two proposals, it seems to me that, because of its broader base, the King proposal is the more important in its implications for improved library services and in its potential benefits to scholarship in general. It does not seem likely that Congress would approve two projects of the same general nature, both of which require unusually large expenditures of Federal funds.

Although the two proposals are different in concept, it might be possible to tie the two together and one question I should like to ask Dr. Warren, therefore, is whether, in the development of his plan, any consideration was given to combining his proposal with that now before the Library of Congress.

On another aspect of the Warren proposal—it seems to me that there might be some disadvantages in locating the program in the MEDLARS office of the National Library of Medicine. If a National Science Library were to be established in MEDLARS it might well develop into a situation in which the tail wags the dog, with a resultant disservice to MEDLARS. There might well be enough advantages in establishing a National Science Library as a separate agency (if it could not be a project of the Library of Congress) to warrant a reconsideration of this possibility.

We all recognize of course that the copyright problems in an undertaking of this kind will be enormous, and I hope tomorrow's panel will be able to give us some possible answers in this difficult area.

Although I have no special reaction to Mr. Freedman's paper, which seemed to have been quite carefully developed, I would like to second Dr. Locke's comments about the need for more economical, more efficient readers, printers, and other hardware. Roll microfilm has been in use since the mid-30s, and we still lack economical and really efficient readers. As a result, many small libraries still cannot afford the readers required to take full advantage of microfilm. As far as microfiche readers are concerned—all those I have seen could be vastly improved.

One final comment. Dr. Osborn's paper made reference to the statement which recently appeared in *Bricks and Mortarboards* to the effect that at Grand Valley State College, Mr. Cornberg "conducted a successful battle to restrict the size of the library to no more than 23,000 volumes." This widely quoted statement does a disservice to librarianship in general and to the librarian and staff of Grand Valley State College in particular. The librarian at Grand Valley has stated on several occasions that no such restriction on the book collection is in effect or was ever considered, and I think the record should be set straight here also.

## Victor A. Schaefer

Coming as I do as the seventh person on the panel, I feel like the seventh man in the batting following all the heavy hitters with no one on base to drive home. Having just completed a new library, I don't exactly fit in either the "committed" group nor the "uncommitted" group. Although the new library building has been occupied since September 18, there is considerable uncommitted space in the building and this could be easily adaptable to the requirements of library automation.

Before I describe the facilities available in the new library at Notre Dame, I would like to comment briefly on Dr. Warren's paper. There is no question on the merits of Dr. Warren's proposal. It has points which stagger the imagination and one in particular which raises a question in my mind is the whereabouts of the manpower required to operate the National Library of Science. Dr. Warren's project has large dimensions and I wonder what the impact will be on the staff of those institutions who wish to participate in this project and how much we will be forced to compete with each other with the kind of expert personnel who will be needed.

Dr. Osborn's comment on the microfiche as a sort of super storage of the journals merits attention. At the same time we probably need more automatic retrieval of the actual microform itself from super storage. The bibliographical control of journal literature by computers does not appear to cause any great problem. But if the demand for printouts from microforms comes as might be expected from a National Library of Science, a rapid selector of material would seemingly be essential.

Since Mr. Freedman is associated with the microfilm industry I'd like to take advantage of his attendance here as a panel member to put to him a question regarding microfilm readers. Unfortunately microfilms are not always of uniform quality because of the condition of the material which is microfilmed, the variations of the microfilm varies from a state of underexposure to a state of overexposure. Yet the microfilm readers are completely inflexible to adjust to the condition of the microfilm. Some microfilm would be more easily read in high contrast, some in low contrast. Could microfilm readers be equipped with a rheostat or other device so that the reader could control the contrast or brightness? The human eye also varies from person to person and the same microfilm might require different kinds of illumination for reading depending upon the eyes of the reader. We can engineer this control for television; why could it not be done for microfilm readers?

Now to the new Memorial Library at Notre Dame and the plans which were made or could be made to adapt the library to automation.

The Technical Services Division occupies nearly 12,000 square feet and nearly all of this space is equipped with underfloor duct work; in addition an area of 1,000 square feet contiguous to the Technical Services Division was specifically planned for automation equipment. This area has a cable directly connected with the Computer Center a short distance from the Library.

The Audio Learning Center of nearly 10,000 square feet is similarly equipped with underfloor ducts containing eight runs on 10-foot centers. Only about one-fourth of the area is now in use. All of this area is adaptable for electronic devices such as closed circuit television and the like. Throughout the first two floors of the Memorial Library, alternate columns are already equipped with electrical channels through which cables can be drawn for automation equipment.

In the high-rise portion of the building, three floors, each having 18,000 square feet, are finished but not equipped. Although planned for future housing for books, each floor has hollow columns adaptable for wiring for automated equipment. The Library has the potential of computer based operations, since it has a cable directly to the Computer Center which is equipped with a Univac 1107, and it is hoped that we would have access on a real time basis.

In fact, between October 1963 and April 1964, some experiments with the computer for circulation control were carried out. It has been suspended because the experiment to determine budget requirements was completed.

To conclude, although the planning for the new Memorial Library was begun in 1958, the building as it now stands is flexible enough so that about 20 percent of the total floor space is adaptable for automated library operations.

George Mallinson

If the preceding speaker feels that he is the seventh man at bat, my position may be that of the fifth appendage on the cow. My experience in the area of information retrieval has been sparse. However, I shall try to avoid being redundant in covering the points of preceding speakers and hope to make a few new observations that seem important. I am a little unhappy about one attitude that I seem to sense in statements of the earlier speakers. Nobody has expressed any joy at the future in our handling of information. There is no "getting up and waiting for the lights to shine." Instead there is a feeling of impending doom, that sometime in the near future we are going to be flooded with awesome amounts of information to jam into awesome numbers of people at an ever accelerating rate. So in the year A.D. 2100, which has been set up as a goal, human beings will be little more than fleshy transmitters of information. If this comes to pass, then I think Dr. Warren's idea of a National Science Library System might as well go down the drain. Instead, we may need a National Geographic Space System that examines and approves applications to use a small share of the earth's space for a computer, a library stack, or on which a child can place his two feet. There may be a question as to whether we will have time or space to go to bed at all to produce the predicted burgeoning population. I certainly don't want to look so pessimistically to a future with such an unmanageable population and enormous bags of information that have to be transmitted that the only hope of solution is for the sun to become a supernova and wipe out our problems quickly.

Again I want to say that I am not sure that I have the right to make some of these comments because of some elements of my background. Right now I am a Graduate Dean. Graduate Deans are frequently known as supporters of obstruction of various varieties and I have been assured on several occasions that the description applies to me. Also I have four children who are absorbing much information and at the same time contribute to the population. I edit a journal whose contents may some day clutter up a ferromagnetic domain of some kind. Worst of all, with reference to Dr. Locke—I come from that portion of the country where little research is going on.

But getting back to Dr. Warren's proposal, I view it in two ways. First it is basically broadening in terms of disseminating information, but it has possibilities of being tremendously narrowing. I think in this latter aspect there is tacit support from Dr. Locke. I refer here to the ideas concerning the glossary, and the standardization of vocabulary. If as I infer from Dr. Locke's statements that we will need some laws to demand compliance to the appropriate input for a computer, I am disturbed a great deal. It has long been known by psychologists and by many others that our present vocabulary is not sufficiently large to cover the realm of ideas we wish to express anything we do. Hence to reduce our ability to express ourselves would not be worth the gain in more rapid dissemination of information. I can't concede that this should be a point of consideration at this conference. There are two specific examples of such restrictive possibilities that hardly can be considered academic and seem worthy of mention here.

Probably few of you have seen the recently-published book by the Seale Company of Indianapolis entitled *I Have a Green Nose Said Zanzibar*. Zanzibar is a red-nosed baboon who insists his nose is green. In front of him he has constantly displayed a plaque reading "Think Green." Now I'd like to know how this is going to be structured in compliance with language for a computer if anyone ever thought it worthy of storage. I'm thinking also of a recent advertisement in *Sports Illustrated*. The theme was simply stated as "It seems there was this cow . . ." I know of no way that we could standardize this vocabulary to get this type of subtlety into a computer.

These may seem to be far-fetched examples, but in my experience as an editor there are analagous ones in many scholarly articles. Standardization of their vocabularies to fit an electronic mind would change a delightful cocktail into warm beer. I would be very hesitant to find our ability to express ourselves either in titles or in abstracts, or in the way we write uniquely, feeble as it is at times, restricted further. Very quickly, our writing would be as homogenized as Howard Johnson has homogenized the appetites of the Eastern seaboard. If we look at this total process of information retrieval, it certainly should not lessen our ability to express ourselves. Neither should it restrict the ways we want to retrieve information. Ideally it should give us greater breadth in the ability to express ourselves, and to perceive the ideas of others. I may not seem to be as concerned as some of you about costs or manpower, or about some other matters of implementation. However, I want to assure you that I am not entirely on the loose end of the stick having come from Michigan where allegedly salaries are seldom paid.

However, matters of implementation should not be restrictive in the design of a system. There are basic matters which should be of more concern, for example, those that are related to the library that we are now planning at Western Michigan University. A few of these are worthy of mention. First of all, the major question concerns, "What is the total scope of a library?" "What purposes is it expected to serve?" "What do you want it to do?" Another question concerns what the purpose of stored information should be. "Is it merely expected to accumulate in some sort of domain preliminary to retrieval?" "Is it the function of the student to push buttons and get information, or is there some broader aim of university education in using stored information?" Assuming there is, then retrieval systems must not be designed as caves in which to store restricted ideas. Rather they should be designed for university purposes. Dr. Warren's Library of Science System may be an excellent way for fostering these purposes.

The system could also be a way of restricting student and faculty initiative because the system demands a specific type of output and yields only a certain type of input. How then are we looking at libraries and potential retrieval systems? Let's look at our present situation. We are committed to a library, but we are committed to remain uncommitted as to the exact design. We are deferring action on a major installation for at least three years and have decided to enlarge the present one. This will provide the time needed to review present technologies and extrapolate the possibilities a few years ahead. Also we'll be able to devote some time to analyzing problems that students have rather than those librarians claim they have.

What are the major student complaints? The main one is that library materials are either lost, on closed reserve or in the bindery. These are the same stories that you have heard before. In brief, rapid access to information is difficult. With greater numbers of students it will become increasingly difficult unless we get multiple copies of journals, meaning more stack space. In any modern system one could hope for technology to provide rapid and ready printouts from journals and serials for every student, without waiting for journals to be returned. Another commitment is that we're not convinced that library materials must be used in libraries or necessarily requested by a student in the library.

Why not use the dormitories for some of the study space that now occupies library space? Western Michigan University may be unique in the number of students it houses, namely, slightly more than 7,000, which is better than 50 percent. During much of the time vast dormitory spaces are empty while students occupy other spaces. As a result we are looking toward possibilities of having printout mechanisms, whatever they may ultimately be, placed in dormitories. This idea, of course, creates complete ruckus among the people involved in housing. They point out that this has never been done before and will create many problems. Unfortunately, they seldom come up with solutions. Naturally such a plan should be viewed as a total university function. What needs to be done to make it total? Will some students be neglected in such a plan? What about those not housed in dormitories? Can consoles used for "requesting" printout be placed elsewhere for these students, and if so, where? How will all this fit into other university purposes? The questions posed have yet to be answered. However, plans are underway in every new dormitory to install enough cable for any system that may emerge. It may of course never be used. But, it's cheap enough to install during initial construction to justify the gamble.

Also it is hoped that a computer with excess capability, whatever that means, may be included in plans for one of the new buildings to handle any electronic retrieval program. This may provide the central storage which may ultimately be useful in some system such as those described by Mr. Freedman or Dr. Warren. Another hope is for the anticipated new library to remain as flexible as possible, with movable partitions and other building features that do not resemble mausoleum architecture. In this way new features and systems can be installed economically and rapidly. I don't know how to do it, but we'll leave that up to the architect. Again I say we are committed to making use of anything that comes out of Dr. Warren, Mr. Freedman or Professor Kent that is good for the University. But we don't want to deal only with what's good for an electronic system's digestion.

### Allen Kent

I'd like to raise a question, perhaps for Dr. Warren. We have gone through the two panels that are concerned with committed buildings: buildings completed and buildings that are far enough in planning or construction so that presumably major changes cannot be made. If I have the sense of the discussion correctly, I think that with relatively few objections there is a passive acceptance of the idea so that if a system such as Dr. Warren's comes about, we will find room for the material, and a way to use it. What, Dr. Warren, do you expect of librarians—of which these are representative? To actively help such a plan; or should they be relatively passive and wait for a plan to emerge and then to have it handed to them?

## Stafford L. Warren

Well, from what I have heard here today and last night, I think there are no passive members here. Everybody has given evidence of a great deal of thought in this direction. Perhaps some feel they would not like to be committed wholly to my proposal at the moment, as the whole thing has a complicated look. I think there has been very careful planning made in individual cases. The problem is not insoluble even if you didn't provide all of the special space for computers. If you have a 15- or 16-foot ceiling, you can still put in a false floor for the electrical circuits; and air-conditioning, and other things without too much expense, to install the computers that would be needed in this first phase at least. I hope that there will be enough support so that the legislation could be passed with some budget to afford pilot programs for those of you who are in this first dynamic and experimental move. The biggest criticism which I have had is that there hasn't been any stir among the professional librarians and this is why I circularized the membership of the Research Librarians Association with my white paper and letter. If the Research Librarians as a group or Association could recommend that something like this be done as a start, then I think we could perhaps unblock most of the obstacles. Some have suggested that a feasibility study be made. I think the time is past for this. MEDLARS and others have demonstrated the feasibility. It's now a technical and organization problem— all solvable with energy and funds *and* a goal. I would like to see the Office of Science and Technology recommend that this be accepted in principle. Then the standards and glossaries should be examined and agreed to through conferences initiated by the Office of Science and Technology which by Executive order has the responsibility to do so. This would be a start in another direction which could be done independently. I think there is enough thinking among the librarians as a whole, that computers will be useful, and that some adaptation will be an improvement over the present situation. I heard Mr. Heiliger's description of how far he has gone with interest because he is approaching this from certain definite segments of his problem and is trying to get an economical solution which will speed up his operation, reduce his manpower, and perhaps his space requirements. It should give a much better service to the students. It is kind of a fresh idea to have a student return to the dormitory to study—this would be very nice. We found in the medical school in Los Angeles that since most of the medical students were married there was too much noise at home and they wanted to study in the library. This changed the concept of the reading space to some extent. It would be nice to see some things like this started to see if they worked efficiently in a different setting. The habits of the students are changeable if the situation is to their liking.

If you can start something with the freshmen without involving the seniors and gradually go through four years, you have got it made. There is no referral to the prior generation to any extent. I don't see any obstacles that can't be solved by ingenuity and improvising changes that will fit your needs. What are your needs? I look at the computer and other such things as tools. Later you may throw them all away. There may be a better system, but it is not here right now. Even if you consider only the time saving and the greater accuracy of the bibliographic search for the faculty and graduate students, then what I have proposed will create a real but intangible and immeasurable saving that outweighs the total cost. One of the big weaknesses at MEDLARS at the moment is that the storage isn't complete. Although it is rapidly becoming very large it's bound to have gaps for some time yet.

If you recall, I divorced the operation of the System from the National Medical Library. The National Medical Library is represented in the Advisory Operating Committee. The present director of MEDLARS or another director would be assigned by the Surgeon General's Office to lead the new program, but all of the libraries themselves still would be left autonomous and intact in their present relationships, with the new responsibility, however, of contributing their tapes from their assigned journals to the pool. One thing that came out of the discussion a little earlier—why not include the titles of books. I have no objection to this except that it just expands the responsibility in this early stage of growth and we need to reduce the problem to as small a level as we can for a few years until the system can be established. If the Library of Congress wants to contribute the titles of books to the pool using their catalogs as a base, after they are computerized, this could be done very readily and I think with very little increase in their new computer catalog system.

## William N. Locke

I'd like to come back to this question of standardization of terminology. Perhaps we are misunderstanding each other as to just what is intended by standardization here. Dean Mallinson mentioned abstract journals. *Chemical Abstracts* has had for 20 years lists of terms which all the abstracters use. This has not, I think, imposed any serious constraints on abstracts. New terms are added as needed. Every library that does cataloging has authority lists. You just can't allow a lot of synonyms to creep in unnoticed or you have trouble. You have to do a lot of cross referencing. When someone asks for something under one name and another under another name, it becomes a foreign language problem and you have to translate. You have to build into your system either standardization or translation. I agree 100 percent that we need to express ourselves. We don't want to tie anyone's hands and prevent them from creating new concepts. Standardization has got to keep up day by day, year by year with the progress of thought in the various fields or it is worthless. Nevertheless you cannot have communication without a conventional medium of expression, without an agreement as to the meaning of terms you are using.

While I have the floor, I want to make two other comments. One is that we have talked a lot about communicating with computers, but the type of computer open to us now is very painful to the human being. I hate to even think of telling our users "you must sit down at a keyboard and type out your questions." The worst of it is that you will quite likely get the answer that such and such is not in the memory or that the computer is not prepared to accept your question. So you figure that perhaps you have not worded your question properly and have to look it up in the book to see how to word it so you can get the answer. I haven't got much better to offer, except in one way. All of us are used to asking a question of librarians in person or over the telephone. Only if forced to, will we write our question out. So, I hope that the day will come (I know it will) when we can ask questions over the phone of the computer. Maybe we won't have to go through the laborious process of typing it, but we will still have to phrase the question right.

## Allen Kent

Don't you think this is just because we are at the beginning?

## William N. Locke

The L.C. Report tells you that when you want to make a search the first question you should ask is how many items you are going to get out in the answer. If it is too many, you rephrase your question. Any librarian would do just as the computer is supposed to do. My point is that we would rather ask our questions orally than have to write them out, and I just want to predict that this will come in the lifetime of some of the people in this room.

The other thing that I'd like to mention is that Bell Telephone is said to be working very hard on this trying to cut the ground out from under the feet of IBM. They are trying to develop computers which will be available on a public utility basis whereby you will simply lease a keyboard in your office or your home or your library and you will have access to a large computer in the local city and even bigger ones further away. In the memories of the computers will be all sorts of programs. Libraries will be in the memories too, so it's perfectly possible that we should not plan, in any libraries that are going to be built ten or fifteen years hence, to put computers in at all. The chances are that we shall see one computer for each university that will take care of all the computer needs, or just one computer in each geographical area which will take care of the needs of the universities, businesses and the inhabitants. I think this is coming very fast.

This enormous change in our computer habits is going to take place in the very near future.

## Edward Heiliger

We are considering the use of the Xerox LDX Scanner-Printer and the Telephone Company's Tel-Pac channels for transmission of not only Xerox copies, but for computer data transmission, voice transmission, and tying typewriters together. Cost figures have been obtained on joining four of the State universities together in this fashion.

## Samuel Freedman

Dr. Schaefer has asked a very practical question about the filing of microfiche. If I interpret the question correctly it refers to the necessity for filing microfiche in jackets to avoid damage in the file. I do not believe it is necessary to file microfiche in jackets although it is possible to do so. Any photographic image is subject to damage and wear and so care should be exercised in handling photographic materials.

Dr. Schaefer also asked whether it is possible to control the brightness of illumination on a reader screen. Not only is this possible but there is at least one reader on the market today with a brightness control built in.

## William N. Locke

This doesn't do anything for contrast, only brightness.

## Edward Heiliger

The National Microfilm Association recently sponsored a study of the effect of reading microfilm on the eyes. The conclusion of the study was that it is a psychological matter. If you think reading microfilm will bother your eyes, it will. If you do not think it will bother them, it does not.

## Samuel Freedman

I think this is true and we have people who sit all day and inspect film. They have been doing it for many years, and we haven't had a problem.

## Andrew Osborn

You asked, Professor Kent, if I would speak on the comparison of the Library of Congress and the National Library of Science program. This is something that interests me very much, and I would really like to think about it to quite an extent before committing myself one way or the other finally. The reason I say it interests me is that in 1940 I found myself participating in a survey of the Library of Congress, then some eighteen months later in a survey of what was then the Armed Forces Medical

Library. The reasons for these surveys and the subsequent history of the two libraries do have quite a bit of light to shed on the relative merits of the proposal.

The occasion for the Library of Congress survey was that Herbert Putnam had expanded the role of the Library of Congress tremendously, developing one important activity after another, yet without the administrative setup to guarantee overall successful operation; his enterprise eventually led to serious difficulties brought about basically by failures in personnel and personnel work. When Archibald MacLeish succeeded him as Librarian of Congress he set to work to try to remedy the situation; and from my knowledge of things as they were in 1940 I am quite sure that a great deal of credit for the rise of the Library of Congress in the past twenty-five years must go to Archie and the tremendous effort he put into the reorganization of the national library. He had the requisite drive and imagination, and in addition he had the strong backing of President Roosevelt.

In some respects the story of the reorganization is one of unbroken success. That is true, for example, of the creation and development of the Processing Department; it is true of the systematic development of the collections. Verner Clapp was put to work to revitalize the whole acquisition program, with the result that from that day to this the Library of Congress has been the most exciting library I know anywhere; it is tremendously stimulating to go there and see the vast quantities of material pouring in from all over the world. The acquisition program alone has been a magnificent achievement, and there has been no turning back or faltering.

For cataloging, though, it is a mixed story. Because of the war it was not until 1946 that progress was possible apart from administrative reorganization and control. In that year *Studies of Descriptive Cataloging* appeared, the result of Seymour Lubetzky's investigations; and it was that work which led, in 1949, to the kind of simplifications in cataloging detail that the 1940 survey had desired. Very curiously, however, these simplifications were promulgated in the very same year that the American Library Association and the Library of Congress jointly published a code whose elaborations to quite an extent ran counter to the simplifications. Unfortunately, some of the simplifications were abrogated this year.

About 1952 Werner Ellinger raised the question of whether the time had come for the Library of Congress to give up subject classification and to adopt a classification by size, a development which the New York Public Library and the John Crerar Library have resorted to in one form or another. The matter received a considerable amount of attention. Maury Tauber of Columbia urged retention of the subject classification for the sake of the libraries which have adopted the scheme. I too wanted to see the Library of Congress continue with subject classification, but felt that a storage library and a storage-library classification were essential counterparts to the successful maintenance of subject classification for some five million volumes or whatever might be the optimum size of the primary research collection. A storage-library program seemed to me to be far more desirable than the Priority 4 scheme which, despite the simplified treatment given to items in this category, applies to important as well as storage-type materials. There are no printed Library of Congress cards for Priority 4 items which can comprise new French literature, new German philosophy, and other works not of first importance for the work of Congress even though they are, for example, for university libraries. So an important source of printed cards disappeared; instead the items are represented in the *National Union Catalog* by typewritten entries, unless they happen to be covered by cooperative-cataloging copy, a contingency that is occurring less and less because the cooperative-cataloging program begun in 1931 is on its last legs apart from the analytics for monograph series.

The progress towards a new cataloging code for the country has been delayed because of uncertainties at the Library of Congress. There was comment at the International Conference on Cataloging Principles in 1961 about the way the American delegation seemed to have its hands tied; and this situation arose because the Library of Congress had not decided in which direction it was ready to go. At the present time the Catalog Code Revision Committee finds that it cannot move in the direction that many other libraries would like because the Library of Congress feels it cannot make certain moves, especially for the names of local bodies, and at the same time it wants more detail as it reverses to some extent the 1940 philosophy and the 1949 gains. At the same time it is something of an anomaly that the 1964 automation report of the Library of Congress will take its cataloging in an entirely different direction.

The point of recounting some of the details of this twenty-four-year period of cataloging history is that for a variety of reasons there have been advances and reverses in the Library of Congress activities, not the steady sure progress one would like to see. And it is for such reasons that I have doubts about the Library of Congress in relation to the program that has been outlined for a National Library of Science, this being to such an extent a matter of bibliographical control.

Now let me present the other side of the picture. I am sure that Dr. Warren knows what the National Library of Medicine was like prior to its reorganization at the beginning of the war. The Army began asking for publications which the library had but could not locate. The Army does not take no for an answer; so a survey which would lead to rapid reorganization was necessary. Much of the difficulty of locating items stemmed from the fact that the catalog cards had no class marks on them. The reference staff had mentally to classify a book as it was requested, then go hopefully to the shelves. There fresh difficulties arose because the books, in the sixty or so broad classes into which the million volumes were arranged, had no book numbers and so might be shelved quite arbitrarily. You will recall the strange old building the library was in. No elevators, of course; a skylight that leaked over the three-tier bookstack whose ranges therefore had been equipped with gutters so the rainwater could run off harmlessly. Primitive conditions of every kind; a really fantastic building. We ought to have pictures so people could see the astonishing contrast in the space of a relatively few years between the old building and the fine modern one in Bethesda, Maryland. Now the big change here—I think this is fair to say —has come from dynamic and imaginative revitalization whose consummation was first MEDLARS and now GRACE. Of course it is a different proposition to recatalog and reclassify a library of the size and complexity of the National Library of Medicine from what would be involved in reworking the Library of Congress as the $70,000,000 for the automation of the catalog records indicates. But even so, or perhaps because of this, I regretfully feel more confident of Dr. Warren's being able to build successfully on a going concern like MEDLARS and GRACE than on the Library of Congress. I say this with very great reluctance and I wish that I could think about it much more carefully than I can on the spur of the moment. Many of my best friends are at the Library of Congress; they are doing outstandingly good work and are carrying a tremendous load. I would most happily find for them and the truly great collections, of science as of other subjects, which they are developing enterprisingly and imaginatively.

The National Library of Science proposal really breaks down into two parts. One is the bibliographical control of scientific literature, the other the textual control; and the immediate tie-in with MEDLARS and GRACE, rather than with the Library of Congress, is on the score of bibliographical control. Actually both are government organizations and therefore fit in with my reading of history that sooner or later the government will have to assume the full responsibility for the nation's indexing and abstracting program, at least in the scientific and technological areas. Today these indexing and abstracting services are at an intermediate stage at which private enterprise is carrying on more successfully than in the past, thanks to an appreciable amount of government financing. The present is fortunately too characterized by a growing measure of cooperation among the indexing and abstracting agencies. The achievements of the moment and of the foreseeable future are impressive and reassuring; but I am afraid that we shall not be able to hold the line unless the government takes over the full responsibility one day.

The Warren proposal interests me greatly on the score of bibliographical control. What I am not so sure about is the textual control. In fact, I wonder whether a totality of textual control is even desirable. For example, as I go around the special libraries I find them reasonably well satisfied with their collecting and service program as long as it is complemented by a prompt and effective photocopying service. When a researcher wants an article which is not in his library, he gets a photocopy as rapidly as may be. The great concern I find among special librarians is over any breakdown in national outlets for photocopying. They point, for example, to the fact that the superbly organized photocopying scheme at the National Library of Medicine is prone to delays, say, on the occasions when required volumes are at the bindery. Deficiencies of various kinds in the national photocopying services have caused some libraries to turn to the Linda Hall Library in Kansas City which is not clogged as some of the national services are and which is able to give prompt delivery. To a high degree then the libraries of the country want a superphotocopying service which in effect the Warren plan would be. Now this is the heart, I think, of Dr. Warren's proposal for textual control that all around the country—and perhaps overseas accordingly—we would be able to get extremely rapid photocopy service; and to this extent I agree most heartily. But to achieve this is Dr. Warren going somewhat too far? What the special libraries need is textual control of journals that are not commonly held. So the question arises, for example, does the *Journal of the American Medical Association* call for computer textual control since it is widely held, both privately and in libraries? Experience in the recently established National Library of Science in England suggests that a service developed to support rather than duplicate textual control has much merit in it.

One of the important factors which has to come to the fore in this discussion is that the Library of Congress is a great general library. If it were a university library it would be able to combine the advantages of the general and special library by having a series of departmental libraries housed separately and administered more or less independently. I cannot emphasize too strongly the enterprise and the vitality that goes with a special library, and the great need that our big general libraries have at times of some of the spirit and drive that the special library can enjoy so much more readily.

My first reaction is that I am very enthusiastic over the bibliographical-control side of the National Library of Science project; I see a great chance of success there. For textual control, though, I wonder whether more limited goals might be equally effective and at the same time be more practicable and less costly.

## Edward Heiliger

Recently we asked the Library of Congress if they would do the coding of their catalog copy for us and supply us with L.C. copy already punched. L.C. refused and suggested that it be taken to some commercial agency. We have since then had a visit from the Head of the Processing Division of the Library of Congress and his favorable reaction to our coding system encourages me to think that there may still be some hope.

## Stafford L. Warren

How can I in my situation help the Library of Congress, because in my proposal I am dependent upon them for a tremendous part of the literature, particularly all the books and many of the journals that are not a speciality of the special library. While I am convinced that the new system should be managed in the Executive Branch, the Library of Congress needs to advance its present program, the computerization of its catalog and the tapes for the journals for the new system, etc. Above all it needs a considerable expansion of budget and a stable growth.

## Edward Heiliger

There is always the possibility that a National Science Library, such as one envisioned by Dr. Warren, could take the responsibility for science materials and that the Library of Congress could develop nonscience materials. However, it seems to me to be more sensible to have all come from one source.

# CHAPTER 8

# UNCOMMITTED LIBRARY PLANNERS

Allen Kent
*(as Chairman)*

We are now ready for the next session and this is the panel of library planners who are not committed in any way.

## Gustave A. Harrer

As I have listened to what we have been saying over the last couple of days, I have noted that we have been talking about several different problems, and you can't comment on them all at one time. I think we were asked to comment on Dr. Warren's proposal which I would say contains two different factors. The first is the national bibliographic control of scientific literature via computer center or centers, and the second is a complete, full-text storage of original text in microform which is supported by Mr. Freedman's paper.

I thought we were further to comment on what we as library planners are doing vis-à-vis electronic development in the field of librarianship. So I will speak on each of these points.

First, Dr. Warren's proposal—Part I—The national or international control of scientific bibliography. In general, I think the proposal is excellent; it is simple; and it is workable, and it seems to answer a seeming need. In several ways, however, I require further data support before I, as a university librarian, can say that I see it as a program of great possible utility to Boston University research programs. I apologize if this is thinking in a small way; I rather think that it is thinking in a practical way. Examples of my questions, without detailing them, are as follows: I would assume that Federal funds cover the cost of experimentation, development, and activation. I would not assume that information is delivered free and/or immediately to all inquirers.

How much will a literature search cost? How soon can the answer be provided? Obviously, the alternative in any situation is to hire a raft of graduate students at varying prices and have them plough through bibliographic resources in the area, or spend the money buying more hard copy original subscriptions. These questions that I suggest could, of course, be greatly detailed and are asked in a gross and general fashion only to get at the nature of my problems.

Based on the information I have, and on the general outline of the scheme, I think the proposal promises a great and practical service to the scientific research community, especially in the future. I say especially in the future because I firmly believe that the anxiety about the control and the need for immediate information is primarily psychological and has been engendered by the apparent availability of apparently miraculous electronic aids—and has perhaps been helped along by the "Madison Avenue" branch of the computer manufacturers.

Part II of Dr. Warren's proposal is the textual pool, and this, it seems to me, is multifaceted. Cooperative ownership and access to current files of thousands of little used periodicals would be a great boon to university libraries. How little used would depend on the institution and the speed of access. The latter point, the speed of access, as I say, needs clarification.

And the need for microformat—Mr. Freedman's argument and conclusions are those of a knowledgeable man whom I respect highly. His task, as he presents it, is to show the feasibility of microform for this purpose with present technology, and this he does. Although I am only a layman in this field, it would seem to me that various other matters might be investigated, given the monstrous space factor. I do not see that the standard reduction ratio needs to be used for the center or centers. Could not the equipment to convert a reduction of 100 : 1 or 150 : 1 to standard size be produced for that purpose, and over the years it would pay for itself?

Mr. Freedman has said that microfiche can best be handled— and as a proponent for microfiche for many years I agree with him entirely—in a manual retrieval situation. I would suggest, however, that this same microfiche format could perhaps be reduced to fit on a 35-millimeter or even 70-millimeter strip of film—could be selected electronically by edge code much more quickly—could not be misfiled—and could be enlarged to standard ratio for distribution, one frame or fiche at a time.

It is, of course, true that under normal conditions, strip film gets badly scratched from running through the reader. This is due to the crude, poorly designed, and I might say, ridiculously high-priced readers presently on the market. Under special, dust-free conditions in a center's laboratories this would not seem necessarily to be the case. In other words, given the size of the proposed project, a minor amount like $1,000,000 or $2,000,000 could develop a lot of helpful equipment.

To progress from there to Dr. Osborn's paper—I believe that Dr. Osborn made some important points. We must distinguish between the various demands on a university library and recognize the differing capability of computers or microforms to answer these demands. His comments point out these differences in a very penetrating way, and cite examples that must not be taken lightly. From my early period as a hopeful and nascent scholar, I could give you a couple of personal experiences to add to his. I hope, however, that no one thinks that either he or I believes that libraries must eschew the advantages of computerization for certain demands, in order to preserve the possibilities of research in such fields as medieval paleography and incunabla printing. The way must be left open for both.

Now, briefly, I would like to proceed to the second question I thought we were to discuss; namely, what do we library planners expect to be the additional demands on our new buildings in the future? What are we doing about it? What do I expect? Specifically, I don't know. I dream of our new building giving no serious problems for about thirty years; but as I reviewed developments over the last thirty years—and feel quite honestly that the library planners of 1934 were almost as enlightened as I—I really despair. I think the best we can do is make educated guesses.

First—The only thing we can really count on is changes, so the building should be physically as completely flexible as possible. Second—I think electrical equipment will be ever more available, so we should provide for the availability of power in any reasonable amount everywhere.

What are we doing? Well, as far as computers are concerned, we did several things. We asked several manufacturers about:

First—the weight—and we found that our floor loading was sufficient.

Second—We asked them about the power required, and we made our conduits large enough and proliferous enough—we hope.

Third—We asked about heat output and found our air conditioning would carry the load. Then we were also told that the trend to transistors helped in all these categories, so the future looks bright.

As for actual computerization of our processes, we are as yet insufficiently impressed with the economy or advantage in service offered by any system presently available to make any commitment. When we are, the building, we hope, will be adaptable.

In audio facilities, we will utilize new equipment in a greatly expanded program, but constructionwise this only means underfloor conduit grid which could carry almost any specific system. Some consideration has been taken of the possibility of closed circuit television from two of our schools to certain areas of the main library building. We will have to wait and see how this develops.

To summarize, we hope that by careful thought we have made the problem of adapting easier for our successors.

## Horace Magoun

It is of possible interest, since we were discussing yesterday the relationship of Federal agencies to Dr. Warren's proposed program, to describe the manner in which the National Institutes of Health are moving into this field of information science. The NIH form a division of the U. S. Public Health Service, along with the National Library of Medicine in relation to which Dr. Warren proposed his national plan should begin. The National Institutes of Health support research and training in the basic medical sciences and health professions; and one of them, with a categorical interest in the Neurological Diseases and Blindness, has a special concern with human communication and its disorders. It seems especially appropriate, therefore, that the National Institute for Neurological Diseases and Blindness (NINDB) plans to move into this field with the establishment of information centers around each research program of a significant dimension in the country. These information centers are designed to take advantage of the resources of the research center and each will be focused upon the focal area of investigation to which the research facility is devoted. A mosaic of information centers will thus be established through the country, which collectively will cover the broad field of the Institute's interest. Integrative effort at the national level will provide for coordination and integration; and these information centers will, additionally, work in close relationship with the National Library of Medicine. The first step in their establishment lies in developing means by which the information stored in the Honeywell computer tapes of the MED-LARS program can be converted into the IBM or other computer systems which are more common in the university settings. There are currently, I think, three or four such information centers which have been or are now being negotiated through contracts with NINDB. One at Columbia is concerned with Parkinson's disease and disorders of movement. One is developing at Hopkins in the area of human communication. One is currently being contracted for at UCLA in the basic neurological sciences. Others exist or are in planning in the fields of epilepsy and cerebrovascular disease.

Each has so far developed a rather common type of starting program. An initial effort is made to survey the user's needs, because there has never been an extensive analysis of how scientists prefer to get their information and how they would like to improve its retrieval. An early step, too, concerns the preparation of glossaries, index headings, and other semantic and linguistic aspects of the program designed to facilitate the recovery of documents and their contained information. These preliminary steps form the primary area of emphasis of specialists in the library field. The scientist is interested in these activities chiefly as they contribute to or expedite his attempt to extract information from the documents retrieved. Having extracted this information, his goal is to utilize it in the preparation of periodic reviews or surveys, which can feed back into his own research or be communicated to his fellow scientists or to other persons to whom it may be of interest.

I would make reference further to only one part of an earlier discussion which had to do with the preparation of standard glossaries, because there is one area of experience which points to the reasonable expectation that this kind of effort can be productive. This is in the field of anatomy, which has concerned itself for some time with the preparation of an international glossary of anatomical terms, called the *Nomina Anatomica,* using medieval

Latin as a universal language of learning by which to communicate across the world. These anatomical glossaries are periodically revised at international congresses, the two most recent ones being the *Basle Nomina Anatomica* (BNA) and the *Paris Nomina Anatomica* (PNA). The success of an international glossary in one field of science suggests that this method may be applied across the board and, the year being what it is today, English rather than Latin might now be proposed as an international language. Hopefully, the active move of this country into the field may lead to this development.

## C. Ray Carpenter

I wish to thank those responsible for inviting me to be a member of this seminar. I am not a library scientist. I have learned much during the discussions that will be useful in planning the Hershey Medical Center. The problem which we confront is to conceptualize the configuration of a modern, advanced medical center that will have the potentials for adapting to unpredictable changes and requirements of the future.

I shall be very general because in a planning procedure such as we are following, it is important to work on a general level before becoming specific and getting locked into a restrictive program of planning or premature architectural designs.

Last night we were discussing reactions between libraries and architects. It was proposed that before one can adequately conceive a library in an institution, the library as a whole must be conceived. I proposed, as an academic exercise, that it would be interesting to wipe the slate clean, start with 150 or 200 acres of land, and ask *what kind of institution* should be built and for what purposes? What are the specific objectives? What kinds of people will be served? What will be the character of buildings and equipment? What should the library be in order to fit the institution? This kind of an academic exercise would help us to think beyond the limits of library functions as they are usually considered.

Please permit me to introduce new terms for the glossary that is already too long—a kind of definition of a library: The library is an activity or operation which involves the management and regulation of the flow of selected content or information in a communications network. A library is not only a building; it is a set of complex operations. A library is a network of communications that permeates the whole institution and the community of which it is a part. When we conceive of the library as a set of functions, then we are free to define the place and role of its functions and certain kinds of technologies which may be needed. We need a sound perspective on computer functions in relation to the total configuration of a system of library communication functions.

I think of the library as only the principal center in a communication system. There are other nodes or subcenters. For instance, other nodes of information in the system are the integrative nodes of different sources or inputs of information, the materials of many kinds that are needed.

The image that I am trying to develop for the Hershey Medical Center is of a network of library functions, and I am trying to think of the library as one of the *principal nodes* of information or resources in this network of information which flows from sources to users.

Yesterday we approached the question of how to define the work of a library. How does one determine what each operation should be, and whether or not the operations are being carried out efficiently? Surely there are pluristic criteria for library functions. What are they? The efficiency criterion could be the following: The provision or availability of the right information, in the right form, in the right medium and mode, at the right time and place, for the persons who need the information. If there is the need to know whether or not the library job is being done, I suggest that this pluristic criterion be applied.

The size of the informational content was not included. This may or may not be relevant. The selective processes applied to the accumulation of library resources are extremely important. What operations and materials are the *selection* responsibilities of a library? One of my principal concerns in planning the library for the Hershey Center is that we do not fill space or computer tapes with materials that have little utility. How can we get this *selectivity?* How can the right materials, and only the right materials, be put into a system of information networks? Another general guideline that is useful for generalized thinking is that the most critical interactions are those that occur between *a person and the information.* This is a critical concern, the "interface." The principal "interface" is the interaction between the person, the learner, and the searcher of information with the materials.

I am not talking only about print or books. I am talking about recorded information regardless of the carrier, the language, or the *mode* in which that information is recorded or expressed.

I have recently defined a pathological condition which is known as medium or mode fixation. This is Freudian terminology, but individuals do get *fixated* on specific *kinds of carriers* of information—books, and prints, for example, or on various forms or carriers that we have discussed in this conference. The *total range* of ways in which information is recorded, transported, or transmitted or transformed needs to be the province of librarians. Incidentally, transformation of information is something that needs a great deal of attention.

More pertinent to architectural questions is the interface between the *person and information*. What are the surroundings and their effects? What are the environmental conditions which optimize these critical interactions? How do you put study-learning behavior into a proper envelope? We have talked about carrels. The models in the basement of this building are mere boxes. What specific function should carrels serve? The question of input-output and the various kinds of information should be provided for carrels.

I recently heard described a carrel that had all information on a disease syndrom. It contained books, specimens, models, and technical publications. A student could go to this unit area and find the full range of information on a defined topic or subject.

The conditions are important, for example, in providing for focusing of attention or controlling interference. The interference factors in many kinds of a learning situation are neglected in design. Furthermore, there can be information overload; more information, irrelevant to the subject, that prevents effective learning or understanding. This is another great problem area that needs to be explored.

A guiding principle that I have in mind may be useful. It seems to have special use in planning a whole institution like the Hershey Medical Center. The principle is to move information to people rather than move people to information. This principle may be applied far more economically or efficiently with modern equipment like closed-circuit television than the procedure of having people go to the library.

In this conference, as in many others, we do not have a common frame of reference. The common frame of reference could be *learning and communication theories*. If these two discordant and poorly integrated conceptual systems could be integrated and learned by all of us, then we might have a common language for facilitating thought and understanding. Operation research methods should become familiar and useful to all of us. Operation research procedures are urgently needed for planning of whole institutions, including the library. Operation research involving the Critical Path Method, the inventory methods, and simulation are applicable to library work. In this day we can ill afford to use nineteenth century methods for planning communications systems of a university, a medical center, or other institutions for the twenty-first century. We ought to use the best planning methodologies which have been developed to design the flow systems of people in space, the flow of materials in space and the other problems. These are problems of relevance to the planning of a library. In fact, modern planning could involve the construction of theoretical mathematical *models* as an approach to architectural planning and construction.

We are building a library in a grass plot of 200 acres in Derry Township. It will take us 50 to 100 years to accumulate the rich store of information resources that we need if we use traditional procedures. We are hoping to become symbionts with some of the rich sources of information that have been developed over the last 100 years. The library at Hershey should be interconnected with the National Medical Library. We hope that the libraries of the medical colleges of Pittsburgh, Philadelphia, New York, Yale, and Harvard will be interconnected with the Hershey Center. We hope to provide reciprocal information services.

Another problem that we confront is that 110 miles separate the Medical Center from the host university. A fundamental assumption is that the Medical Center shall be *"university based."* We are proposing to install reciprocally microwave links, or whatever is required, between the university and the Medical Center. Important sources of information may be interchanged with the affiliated hospital. They could have input-output mechanisms tied in with the Center.

This brings me to the question of the place of computers in medical centers. I think this is a very special problem for a task force working specifically on the problem. We at Penn State may be spending $6,000,000 on a new computer center. Do we need to duplicate this at Hershey, or can we tie in the computer capacity at University Park with the Center 110 miles away? This is one of the questions we must explore. I hope that it will be possible for us to tie in with the computer center at the university, however the question of utility, economy, and availability comes up again. In many medical centers the computers that have been installed have been used only 10 to 12 percent of the time, mainly for accounting purposes. Here there is great capacity waste, for patient records, for management functions, for national information exchange could be arranged to use the comuter capacities for which they are appropriate.

Finally, I have two points. First, we have been talking about this weapon and pointing it from ourselves. I suggest we point the computer weapon directly at library functions, and that we launch research programs with computers so directed as to answer some of the questions that were raised here yesterday and today. The question of selectivity and utility rates of various kinds of materials should be investigated. If we have completed records on what has very high utility, intermediate utility, and low utility, then we could get at the question of what is really needed. Is it needed in 10 seconds or 10 minutes, an hour or 24 hours? When these answers are available for the wide range of media or modes, then the implications are clear for the way in which the library structure can operate.

Finally, I would suggest that we need to add to the computer some eyes and ears, that we turn it on the people in libraries. It is a fascinating opportunity to study *the behavior of people in libraries*. Who are they? Where do they go? What do they do? When do they do it? How much time do they spend at it? We need to chart the paths of people in libraries. We should be concerned about when and where they were frustrated and what their reactions were to frustration.

When we see a picture of communication needs with a library of one central node, then we begin to see the possibility of sensible rational effective disbursal of all materials. When we planned the Florida Atlantic University's Information Resources Center, the library was only one part of the Center. We thought of three areas of access—*immediate, intermedial,* and *remote* areas—for the materials. This assumed that the material had to be carefully classified. I like to think of it as *diamond* space, *gold* space, and *silver* space. The values of spaces and the functions served in them should be correlated. Only materials of high utility and value should be designed into diamond space.

## Allen Kent
*(as Chairman)*

I guess one of the most difficult tasks is that of the architect who has to react to undefined needs for an undefined future, and Mr. Swinburne has been kind enough to agree to so react.

## Herbert Swinburne

As one of those, like Ray Carpenter, who is not a librarian (although Ray is an educator), I don't know whether I am sad or glad to be alone.  Mr. Carpenter just said that a library is not a building, and now I'm asked to discuss the library building.  According to his jargon, therefore, I am discussing nothing.

Dr. Harrer wants the building for thirty years with no problems, and I can assure him he is not going to get it.  I understand that you lose one card in a hundred in the Library of Congress.  That is an error of 1 percent. I think that you should expect at least an error of 1 percent from your architect, and it will probably run to 2 and 3 percent including walls that don't move—of course, there shouldn't have been walls there in the first place. I also speak not just as an architect but as architect-planner, for reasons that will become obvious in a moment.

I'd like to say I am here four years too late.  I think this conference is four years too late; it is too bad this new concept of library information science initiated here at the university didn't happen a long time ago.

Let me speak only about designing a library.  I am not competent to talk on Dr. Warren's report.  But let's take something Dr. Waarren said, "It has to be simple . . .;" Professor Kent said, "You have to be practical," and Mr. Freedman said, "You have to be available," and this morning Mr. Carpenter said, "You have to be specific."  I'd like to add some words here.  Say we are going to deal with space and creativity and people and imagination, and this implies a total system that I have been hearing so much about around here.  When you design a library as a planner, I say that you must begin with a larger frame of reference than the library.  You begin with a total concept of the university and the philosophy of the mission of that university, and then you begin to see how the library fits into this total concept.  Don't get too self-oriented as you examine the position of the library.  Be just a little generous as you see positive areas of overlap. Nodes, if you will, can conflict too.  You also examine the next lower frame of references which is interior space. Interior space and connections within this space. You cannot design helter-skelter, room by room. You must go further with operation programming and research, because you must consider how people are going to interact within this interior space. Concurrently with architectural design goes interior design, which includes all the gadgetry and minutiae that occur in the individual spaces.

In the design of all buildings in relation to higher education we try to find some common concepts in them that run through all the buildings. The library is one of these buildings. We are involved with a student and faculty, and we are going to have some resources to care for. We are going to say that they are all united in terms of curriculum. The students are involved in learning; the faculty are involved in teaching, and some of these resources, as I tried to picture for this group here, were servo systems. I understand now these are not servo systems, but rather, media and mode. The interface between student and faculty is human reaction. Student-faculty contact and the area between that interface is student contact. I would like to suggest that we also have student-electronic contact, and this involves the entire field of human engineering which is so overlooked. I will come back to that in a moment. Between the faculty and his systems are the technicians who are going to help the poor fellow with all the gadgetry that we are discussing. The architect begins with this, and in the library I suppose we are going to eliminate the faculty—as a teacher, he will be a user of your facility. We are involved with a library and a learning process. A library, like many structures in your university, consists of spaces of all kinds, and these will be filled with complex equipment—or servo systems.

The library ought to be a place where a student can meet all this gadgetry happily, and he can't do it within the present state of the art because the human engineering concept hasn't got down to uniting man and machine happily. The library, as I see it, ought to be student oriented. It is an environment for learning, not teaching. The library is an educational space, a social space and a contact space; and it is now going to be filled with gadgetry that I will simply refer to as black boxes. The concept of the black boxes is your responsibility; how the black box gets built into a specific space is our responsibility; but neither of us can go it alone. We must both work with each other, and I am sure that tomorrow these black boxes will be more in number and will be fantastically complicated. As for me, the library will remain a place for books, and black boxes. Instead of getting smaller, it will get larger. You will have to do all the things that you are doing today, and then you will have to add to it all these black boxes. It would be interesting to know what each one of you thought—who should control the black boxes and the computers? I do believe we might consider this as a total university problem and not just a library problem. There is some conflict in my mind, too, as to the overlap between your black boxes and similar ones that are in communication centers and are concerned with audio-visual techniques, television, and so on. Solutions to your problems should fit the total university concept, and when you mold your concepts with others in the institution then the university and the student are better off.

I think Dr. Osborn mentioned this in his paper that the concept of humanism in all structures of the university, and particularly the library, can't be overlooked. It is not an antiseptic structure, easily maintained, priced at so much per square foot for this and so much for that. It must be warm and inviting, not be hard and glistening. I would like to come back to the connectors that I mentioned. The series of spaces that exist in your building or any other building on a campus are reached by connectors. These corridors, usually, are terrible things, and the concept of how to move pleasantly from one space to another needs a great deal of research. The same is true of your exterior connectors. We need what we sometimes call "people pockets." We need internal people pockets. We need places to develop contact and it can't be done with corridors 200 feet long and tile walls and tile floors. This truly is the nervous system. The concept of perception of space is not a visual experience alone. The development of other forms of special perception must be considered. Some fragmentary studies are being made in this direction. Your building will be much more useful if you just keep in mind that there is more to it than visual perception. Ray Carpenter spoke about studying the behavior of people in libraries. If only some architects could understand some of the behavioral sciences and how people react in particular environments and to each other, we might get better buildings and better libraries. I also like to think there were a couple of mistakes so it won't be a superhuman mechanism that is superperfect. I think a perfect environment might not necessarily be a good environment. We once did a dormitory and were told we had to reduce it to the absolute minimum, because they couldn't afford very much. We were a little fearful, so we decided to build a full-sized mock-up of a dormitory room and run students of both sexes through, the faculty deans, and so on, which we did. We juggled this and juggled that. We got the most efficient piece of space you ever saw in your life; but it's too small. It all fits; it all goes in, and they are all satisfied but ten years later they wish it was a foot longer or wider; and I do too, but if we made it like that in the first place we could have never finished it, because it would have cost too much money.

We once designed a student union building and employed this human concept, if you want to call it that. We decided that it ought to comprise a lot of quiet spaces instead of a lot of noisy spaces. The place is a great success and they petitioned the university to leave it open late at night so they can study there. Interaction can be developed in the most peculiar spaces. It should be developed in dormitories and in student unions as well as in the library.

If only we could get human engineering to help us get a person and a machine together in a way where the person is happy and the machine efficient. Architects can't always do it for you; and just to talk about the glare or contrast in the viewer is only one aspect of the problem. We saw yesterday or the day before how IBM consoles are being made more foolproof by having less gadgets on the outside. Symbiosis is not a new word—but its concept in building is new. I would watch out for electronic carrels in libraries, because the carrel as I see it is a glorified desk where you get privacy and quiet. It is a place where you can sit down and be alone. I wonder what this would do to the inside of a library if we had a hundred of these things going at once with all the noise that they can generate?

I wish you would turn the human engineer loose in your computer center; if you won't do that, turn me loose. The first thing that you're conscious of when you enter is the noise. Of course, everyone is so proud to get this gadgetry today that he displays it. It isn't a work area alone, it is an exhibition area as well. But to impress the visitor, you show it all at once; and it is hard and shiny, noisy and whirring, bright and glistening. There is no change in texture, no change in color, no fragmentation of space. You ought to put up some space dividers that would absorb sound, stop vision and take your eyes off tapes and printers and buttons and knobs. You could spread a carpet down even if you had to clean it once in a while. There are so many things you could do in a computer center to make it quieter and more pleasant space. You should stop making it a great big marble showplace.

How do you proceed? Well, first comes the master plan—and you had better not build a library until you have a master plan, which is a joint venture that begins with programming. You should have this as well as your educational library program and special program. You should have an operation program and an environmental program. It should have flexibility; but we all say that and go quickly on to the next subject. Remember, too, that flexibility is three-dimensional as well as two-dimensional. A low ceiling height complicates a lot of things. The changes that are going to occur and make the building give you problems thirty years may be caused by low ceiling heights. Flexibility is expensive. You should define limits and not leave it up to your architect. There are certain areas in your building that will require electronic accessibility. You should do more than put in walks, underfloor ducts, and provide for electronic flexibility. You ought to think in terms of "total walls" or "total riser systems" rather than merely putting in conduits.

As you people become more involved with this kind of gadgetry you're approaching the complexity of medical science buildings, and you are going to need more money per square foot to give you this degree of flexibility and expansibility. We seem to be satisfied with a budget that runs around $25 a square foot, but we wish it were $30 or more. A building to house and operate all your black boxes will run much more.

If we are going to have excellence in education and excellence as you challenge us in this new information process, you still must have excellence in the heritage of books and written words. You must also have excellence in your black boxes, computers, data, and speed. This will require a warm human quality in your architecture, and a respect for the dignity of the people who work in or use the building. This is the only way you attain an enriched educational input of the library into the total university system.

Let me challenge you people on one thing. I don't know if it is going to work, but when I saw that computer and data plotter analyzing some high school essays, I was fascinated. Why don't you get a few thousand-word essays on what an ideal library should be from these librarians in attendance here and put them in that machine? I'd like to see what comes out in the way of a plot. It might indicate juxtaposition; it might indicate proper relationships; it might indicate design direction, and so on.  If the output is logical, I will design a library building for you based on these essays.

## Allen Kent

In listening to Dr. Harrer and recollecting Jack Moriarty's comments that he will not tolerate in his university more than one system, I am curious to learn whether there are any specialized information activities going on in Boston University, sort of under your nose, that react to a problem which the library is not reacting to.

## Horace Magoun

One such activity in the Boston area is the Neurosciences Research Program, of which Dr. F. O. Schmitt of M.I.T. is chairman. The program is sponsored by M.I.T., but operates out of the American Academy of Arts and Sciences, rather than at a library or other institution.  Its goal is to some degree like that of the Information Center program supported by the NIH and perhaps it has some NIH support.  Information is exchanged through the association of some 20 or 30 leaders in the field of molecular biology as this relates to the neurosciences.  It has operated so far largely by the pre-circulation of papers, supplemented by periodic conferences or symposia reported in a loose-leaf, lithoprinted bulletin.  In addition to this nonspecific goal of information exchange, the neurosciences program of Dr. Schmitt seems to possess a more special purpose of active research promotion. The association of a small group of working scientists, communicating their most current advances to one another, before publication in the general literature, appears designed to stimulate and facilitate scientific progress, in much the same way that the seventeenth-century Italian and French Academies and the English "Invisible College" did, before the establishment of more elaborate and formally organized scientific societies.

## Allen Kent

This Neurosciences Research Program of F. O. Schmitt is just one example of the proliferating specialized information centers.

## William N. Locke

It is not an information center.  Let me talk about it unless you know about it.

## Allen Kent

I have served as a consultant to them. There are many organizations that may not call themselves specialized information
centers, but which nevertheless might be identified as such by
a definition imposed from elsewhere.

## William N. Locke

This is not an information center, in the sense in which people
usually talk about information centers. Will you define the sense
in which this is an information center since you have consulted
on it? How and why do you call it that? Just exactly what do
they do that makes you call them an information center? I am
not quite sure it is not a lot of other things.

## Allen Kent

May I suggest a very practical way of defining a specialized
information center. After the Weinberg Report of January,
1963—one of whose recommendations was that specialized information centers development shall be fostered—many organizations approached various government agencies for funds for the
development of specialized information centers. The definition
of a specialized information center, with tongue in cheek, is one
that procures money from government organizations for that
purpose.

## William N. Locke

I don't accept that—not for a minute. Knowing how at random
some of these decisions in government turn out to be. I certainly
will not accept that as a definition.

## Allen Kent

I don't accept it either.*

## John H. Moriarty

I want to talk about whether there should be one or two or
more groups working on this. Roy, you were fabulous. I have it
all written down. You wanted pluralistic critique and you came

---

* A thorough discussion of this point is given in Allen Kent (ed.), *Specialized Information Centers* (Washington, D. C.; Spartan Books, Inc., 1965).

up with a provision for availability and these are your words: "The right information in the right form in the right medium at the right place and time"—then you added—"for the person who wants it." You didn't say for the "right" person who wants it. You didn't say that. You should have. Now if at 20 minutes to 9 o'clock I am patrolling the floor out in the reading room and a person grabs my arm and says: "I want something special on cancer," I know he is a freshman going to give a talk to his speech class in 20 minutes. I lead him over to the Encyclopedia Americana and go on my way. And probably he is no longer in a dilemma. He will have his four points for his speech at 9 o'clock. On the other hand, a rather haggard young man of twenty-eight comes around and says: "Where is the stuff on cancer?" I am likely to say: "You are in the wrong place." But I will take him over to the index cases and I will show him where he can find the general material. I will also say: "Why don't you go down to the veterinary library?" He disappears and the Vet Librarian calls me up: "What is this physiology major doing down in my place?" Well, I remind him that every student is entitled to use every bit of material on our campus; her library is not just for Vet majors. "Well," she informs me, "this student has just got everything we own and he wants to borrow it all." I will say, "Lend him what you can and tell him to come back to read the rest." Now this is what I really mean by having one system on a campus; but I also illustrate the fact that the reader is the person for whom this service is right, and I think both he and we have to take some responsibility. Speaking as a group of educators, we have to take the responsibility of adjusting the material to the student. Just as you tell them how to use the streetcar system, you have to start them when they are boys to use these intellectual works like a system. They have to be "right" for their problem.

Allen Kent

But Jack, the streetcar system is going out.

John H. Moriarty

But you have to pick it up. There is a transfer there.

Horace Magoun

I have one more comment to Bill Locke. I insist on being practical with regard to the specialized information center field. I agree that many people who perhaps are individual scientists, groups of them who get involved in pieces of activity that really aren't educational centers at the start, get empty buildings before very long. With the availability within the NINDB and many others, suddenly it is somewhat of a monstrous thing, overlapping activity in other areas. You can't turn your back on it; it is a practical consideration. I insist on it.

## William N. Locke

I agree entirely, but this thing we are talking about is a group of specialists in one field communicating with each other, keeping each other up to date, getting together once in a while, writing papers for each other's approval and probably eventually publishing them. They have called it a "college without a campus." To some extent it may act as an information center. On the other hand, they don't have much of a library as far as I know. I don't know to what extent they serve other people. It is my impression that they do not allow others, only members of their own groups, to have access to the information. You can't call that an information center.

## Allen Kent

Well, there are several waves to this. There is a central core of the program. Then there are ways of radiating information out from it. Not being a neurosurgeon or in any way involved in this field, I still got material from them. I don't ask for it. It is automatically radiated out from them.

## Horace Magoun

I think we need to do more in the analysis of what Mr. Swinburne called human engineering, as this applies to user's needs. These two patterns that we have been discussing may represent two distinctive categories of need, which will require differential rather than common solutions. In response to one of them, the pattern of information centers, now being developed through NINDB and other agencies, is designed to satisfy the need with which the library field has been most interested. Its effort is directed to getting appropriate information out of chaos and into the hands of users with dispatch, so that when someone is preparing to review a subject, he won't have to spend half of his time rummaging around the library to collect the documents out of which he needs to extract and synthesize the relevant information for general exchange.

Another need is to communicate the inevitably chaotic frontier of a rapidly moving field of research to closely related workers, in different places and in different areas of the field, who can profit by the stimulation and reinforcement of association with one another. Its effort is directed toward the special promotion of creativity in research, which is a quite different goal from that of preventing the waste of half your time collecting information for review.

An earlier instance in the Boston area, before the current program in the neurosciences, about which both librarians and architects might wish to think, involved the luncheon meetings which brought together Arturo Rosenblueth, associated with Walter Cannon and other physiologists at Harvard Medical School, who were interested in the feedback control mechanisms regulating homeostasis in body processes; and Norbert Wiener, and some of the young people in mathematics and engineering at the Massachusetts Institute of Technology, who were interested in the feedback control processes involved in servomechanisms in engineering. This was an enormously stimulating and creatively productive association, out of which developed the concepts of cybernetics, concerned with the basic features of control and communication in the animal and the machine, which have since been extended to many fields.

I was pleased to hear Mr. Swinburne make reference to the construction of "people pockets" in buildings, designed to foster the communication of ideas rather than of information in the technical sense. From the point of view of advancing the field of knowledge, this communication of ideas may be far more important in the long run than the saving of 50 percent of a person's time spent in collecting information.

## Allen Kent

Thank you, Dr. Magoun. Mankind will always use anything that ever worked well for him and certainly personal communication has always been a magnificent means.

## Edward M. Heiliger

Ray Carpenter's remarks reminded me of a comment made by one of General Electric's information men when he looked at our card catalog at the University of Illinois. He said, "This is a delayed message center." It is true that the catalog is full of messages about messages. The object of the catalog is to guide future readers to the original messages, which may well have been written with no thought of the reader of the distant future. The whole university is, of course, a message-exchange center. The professor is delivering messages to the students by word of mouth and by the use of various audio and visual aids. In our institution, each professor will have at his back an 8 × 10-foot screen and his lectures will be preprogrammed so that he can call onto the screen or through audio facilities messages other than his own to assist him. In our library, the messages about messages which constitute our catalog will be filed on a computer tape. I think that consideration of the concept of the university as a message center makes the whole communication picture become a little clearer.

CHAPTER **9**

# COPYRIGHT

J. H. Kuney

It would be silly to discuss how much of the copying that is going on is in violation of the copyright law. We could argue about it. We could discuss it for many months and we would reach no conclusion.

We should be aware of the fact that until such time as the courts have ruled on each and every facet of copying procedures no one can do anything but speculate as to the amount of copying which is or is not in violation of the copyright law. From what we have observed in the eight or nine years we have been studying this problem there is no evidence that anybody is anxious to test this thing in the courts. I think each concerned party is afraid of an adverse court decision.

There are a couple of factors that are mitigating against court action. As publishers we have as yet no real evidence which would be useful in court or even in discussions that there has been any damage to our ability to publish. Secondly, we can only speculate as to the amount of copying that might be in possible violation. Libraries, such as you represent, have been cooperative and willing to make studies, but in the areas where we are probably more concerned—that is, industrial libraries—we are not about to get the kind of cooperation needed to analyze the problem.

I think it might be worth repeating here something we are all quite aware of and which Dr. Osborn made very clear in his remarks. It is the efficiency and economy of copying techniques that have created interest in this problem, that is, the copyright problem. And we think it is significant that the original concern

167

which has been manifested has come primarily from those who manufacture copying equipment and from those who are doing the copying. You have heard less from publishers on this problem than you have from the other two sides. And what the publishers have said about the copying matter has really been an attempt to answer the questions raised by the other two groups.

We need to be aware that if the problem continues in its present direction we are not too far away from the time when some of these issues will be tested in the courts. I don't know who will do the testing, the users or the publishers. We certainly have no plans, but I think perhaps it might be worth calling to your attention a very recent court decision rendered on August 12, 1963. It is the Addison-Wesley Publishing Company versus Brown, doing business as University Science Publications. Some of you may have read about this case in *Publishers' Weekly*. It involved a group of professors who prepared a set of answers to a set of books by another author and who were selling the book of answers separately from the original book. The courts ruled that this was an infringement of the copyright of the original publisher of the book. I'd like to read to you one paragraph from the court decision which may prove significant:

> Textbooks and scientific works present special problems and require special treatment in applying doctrine of fair use; those who for their own requirement avail themselves of instruction given in texts or who apply the art described therein do no more than act upon the license the author grants and do not thereby infringe; however, another's use of same methods of statement, whether in words or illustrations, in a book published by other for teaching the art infringes copyright. . . .

It is possible that here are words which might keep cropping up in future activities about copyright violation, and I feel it is involved in some of the things we have heard about here. I don't think there is much question that a scientist or an individual who wants to make a copy for his own use is not in violation of the copyright law. I would not attempt to say the microform described here is a violation of the copyright law, but I do think we are beginning to get to the borderline of this problem. Again it will be the courts that will have to decide and I think these things will come to the courts eventually. Probably, they will be brought piece by piece, little aspect by little aspect, until finally some pattern emerges which might become a basis for decision.

The copyright law is scheduled for revision but there is no evidence that anything is going to be in the revision of the copyright law that's going to solve our problem. There is only one very real problem and that is the publishers' ability to publish. It is in fact part of your responsibility to see that you do not deprive the source of primary information of its ability to continue to function. Somehow it must be paid for. In almost all the numbers that we have seen used in connection with the cost of information retrieval, it is assumed that the primary information, whatever its form, is available at zero cost.

It would seem useful to an understanding of this problem if I gave you a little background as to what the American Chemical Society does in its publication program. During 1964 we will spend in excess of $10,000,000 producing journals, including *Chemical Abstracts*. We produce 18 journals in addition to *Chemical Abstracts*, and I think it is important to understand that the basis of the publication program is the willingness of over 97,000 chemists and chemical engineers to support the publication program through their membership in the ACS. Part of every member's dues goes to the support of the program in addition to the money that is paid as subscriptions. There is a recognition by the scientist that he has a responsibility to support publications in his area of interest. In addition to the dollar output, a tremendous amount of volunteer labor on the part of scientists in reviewing papers, in preparing abstracts, and in the writing of papers, goes into cur scientific publishing program.

Further, we need to be aware that there has been a tendency to develop journals that are more specialized in content and audience. This is not the place to discuss whether the journals are becoming more specialized as the leader or as the follower. The chances are that the journals are following the activity of the researcher, and since the work of the scientist has become more specialized the journals have become more specialized. Where once stood the single *Journal of the American Chemical Society*, there are now 18 journals serving a variety of specialized fields. The trend is likely to continue in this direction. We see that for the immediate future that the tendency will be to produce more journals each dealing with an ever narrower slice of scientific discipline.

We operate all our journals as near as possible on a long-range break-even point. In other words, if we make money one year, we realize that somewhere along the line we will have deficits. It is also relevant to be aware that journals serve two purposes: current awareness and retrospective searching, and some of the problems that we have talked about result from failure to recognize that these two are separate and really quite different techniques. Our thinking is pointed primarily at the current awareness need, although the design and the care that goes into journals is in a large part recognition of the fact that the journals we produce are part of the permanent literature.

It is important also to be aware that the American Chemical Society and many other scientific societies are doing much research in the field of how to do a better job of journal publication. The Chemical Abstracts Service has a large research group which is seeking to determine the role of computers. In Washington we have a project dealing with computerized typesetting. Clearly, libraries can begin to think about getting journals on tape. Within the next five years we are going to see more and more of this and I think it is not too soon. One of the things I'd like is to encourage you to think about how you would use information that was available to you in machine-readable form.

One of the concerns we have about Dr. Warren's proposal is the conflict or rather the need for bringing some kind of order between mission-oriented information centers and discipline-oriented information centers. Whether a National Library of Science can meet both needs or whether the design is even concerned with both needs, I don't know. Our own experience is that the mission-oriented groups are already very well entrenched and that it looks to us as though part of the problem is going to be to match the needs of discipline-oriented centers with mission-oriented centers.

One question I would ask is: What can a National Library of Science do that cannot be done now? One feeling I get is that you as librarians see in a National Library of Science a method of relieving yourselves of some of the storage problems of handling marginal journals. This may be a useful and desirable function, and if it is a legitimate and needed function, a method of fulfilling the need will certainly develop. I don't think that is enough to merit calling it a National Library of Science.

We are disturbed also about the nature of the indexing and abstracting problem that seems to be hidden below the surface of the National Library of Science program. The ACS of course has a very large vested interest in indexing and abstracting services and we have just completed, or we are on the verge of completing, a new building in Columbus which will have about 185,000 square feet of floor space and house in excess of 700 employees concerned only with the operation of the Chemical Abstracts Service.

We need to consider also the role of the government in activities requiring editorial evaluation. Under government operation can we maintain the editorial quality and regard for user need toward which our discipline-oriented societies strive? At this moment I fail to see that it will be possible under the conditions in which it must operate for a single government group to give editorial direction to a variety of scientific disciplines. Further, the government has given increasing evidence that if you are going to take government money, you are going to dance to the government tune. Admittedly, when the question of copyright comes up, the government would be a worthy opponent in any kind of court battle.

As we see it, at least for the moment, we will have to rely heavily on the quality of our product and the importance of the contribution that science makes to the culture and the society as a whole for maintaining our position in the communication picture.

## Allen Kent

In the Addison-Wesley case, were any damages awarded?

## J. H. Kuney

I don't know. An injunction was issued enjoining the defendants from infringing the copyrights of the plaintiff Addison-Wesley. Any further relief was to be decided at a later hearing.

## Elmer Hutchisson

I would like first to supplement some of the things Mr. Kuney had to say particularly from the point of view of a journal publisher. Obviously science is a cooperative enterprise and it is the task of professional societies such as the American Institute of Physics to assist in providing good communications between those who are participating in this cooperative enterprise. To a physicist there is no information explosion. When one speaks about an explosion one means an uncontrolled expansion. There isn't any uncontrolled expansion, at least in the field of physics. Although growing, the number of pages of research reports published per year is proportional, over a sixty-year period, to the number of workers in the field of physics. Sixty years ago there were about

200 physicists and about 200 pages per year were published; fifteen years ago there were about 10,000 physicists and 10,000 pages a year; now, there are about 40,000 physicists and 40,000 pages are published per year. In other words, one physicist publishes, on the average, one page per year. Also, the amount of research published in the American physics journals depends upon the amount of money that the government spends upon physics research. From the total research expenditures we can estimate the amount spent on physics very closely year after year. We find that for every page of our journals approximately $10,000 has been spent on research and this figure has remained approximately constant over the last few years.

Physicists operate on a philosophy that publication is part of the cost of doing research since no research is really useful until the results are published. It is, therefore, very proper that the organization sponsoring the research should assist in the publication of that research. This is done by means of what we call a "page charge." For every article which is accepted for publication in our journals, the institution supporting the research is asked if it will pay a charge proportional to the number of printed pages. Actually, the payment is voluntary since the paper is published whether or not the payment is made. In fact, the editor does not know whether the charge is paid or not, but the great majority of the organizations do pay and a large part of the cost of publishing the journals comes through the sponsor of the research.

The policy of page charges has made it possible for individual physicists to be able to afford their own copies of physics research journals. We believe that this practice is important for the progress of science. The sharing of the publication cost has also been very helpful to libraries since they are able to purchase these journals very cheaply. Libraries can buy, in the field of physics, all the American journals which the American Institute of Physics publishes which are essentially all the physics research journals published in America for $272 per year. For this, the library receives 16 journals containing approximately 40,000 pages a year and these pages are of large format, with about one thousand words per page. In other words, the cost to the libraries is less than one cent per page for these large size pages. Of course, 40,000 pages per year takes a lot of space. I must admit that storage is a problem but the actual cost of the journals is not very great.

In saying that there is no information explosion in physics, I don't mean that there are no publication problems. Mr. Kuney has mentioned that one of the problems we are becoming increasingly concerned about is the fact that our physics journals, over the years, have been designed by physicists for physicists. They are organized strictly in terms of the interests of physicists. We have, for example, a nuclear physics journal, or an acoustical, or an optical, or chemical physics journal since these are the areas physicists specialize in. But, with the breaking down of the barriers between the disciplines, it is clear that not only do the physicists use physics journals but so also do biologists, engineers and other project-oriented groups. How can we serve these broader areas? Since we believe that it is part of our responsibility to attempt to serve them better, we have been conducting documentation research for the past several years. The AIP research program ties in closely with other programs such as that of Mr. M. M. Kessler of M.I.T., who is working with Professor Locke. One problem we are considering is the possibility of an alerting system in which we would publish monthly a list of titles or extended titles of all the articles published in AIP journals. The list would appear simultaneously with or even before the journals themselves. The titles would be classified into broad areas and carry code numbers. From an interest profile of various workers in related fields, we could find out which titles a person would like to have. Shortly after the journals are printed, separates could be produced which, by the use of a computer, would be addressed to the interested people. In this way we could send out tailor-made packets of physics literature to anybody who wishes them. Alternatively, they could use the periodic classified title list as a sort of a mail-order catalog and order by serial numbers the exact separates they want. Such a tailor-made service would be expensive. It turns out to be more expensive to send out 10 separates on specific subjects wanted than some 10,000 pages of standard material. If we could train physicists to read journals like they do the *New York Times* and tear out the things they are interested in and throw the rest away we probably wouldn't need a separate service. However, because journals are nicely bound, physicists like to keep them intact and we have to find some other way of giving them just the material they wish.

I am sure that libraries will continue to have all of the literature on physics, because there is such a variety of demand that they have to satisfy. The individual's interests are more specialized and he would prefer to receive only what he wants to read. Some day we hope to be able to provide this service at not too great an expense. What I have been saying is in the nature of an introduction to my real assignment.

The question that really concerns us this morning is the violation of copyright in the Warren proposal under discussion. Do such violations harm the institutions, which in their cooperative way, publish the results of research? The American Institute of Physics, like the American Chemical Society, is a nonprofit organization. As I see it, there are at least three potential ways in which we might suffer. One would be loss of subscription income. This is actually not a very large item because, as I mentioned, we have page charges. We attempt to set the page charges so that they will cover the entire cost of composition and editorial work. We try to include all costs before we begin running the presses. Since we operate on a nonprofit basis, the subscription price needs to cover only the cost of running off copies. In this manner if the number of subscriptions decreases, the printing cost decreases a similar amount and thus we really are not terribly concerned as to whether or not the number of subscriptions goes down. It is obvious that they can't go too far down because then the efficiency would decrease and the unit cost would go up.

Let us consider the next item. The income from back issue sales is considerable. For one of our journals, the *Journal of Chemical Physics,* we receive some $20,000 annually from back issue sales. This is actually about 5 percent of the income for this journal. The charge that we make for reprints in usual quantities is about 2 cents a page. About one-half of the income is credited to the production cost of the journal, thus reducing the income which we have from the sale of back issues. If we provide reprints through photocopying, the cost also would be approximately a cent a page. This is just a very rough guess but I should think, reasonable.

The loss of advertising is another factor. As you know the advertising charge per page depends upon the number of subscriptions. If the number of subscriptions is influenced then our income from advertising goes down. It is very difficult to estimate what this would be, but we do know the advertising income we receive from each text page of our journals. The best estimate I can make roughly is that again we would lose about a cent per page from our advertising income for every article that is photographed and given out by libraries.

In Dr. Warren's proposal it was suggested that possibly the losses of the nonprofit professional societies could be made up by stamps which would be affixed to photocopies or, alternatively, by the outright purchase of photocopies to be placed in an inventory. As I mentioned, the AIP is considering the possibility of off-prints or separates. We could sell these directly to the library so that they, instead of photocopying, could provide off-prints. This would be a simple way to solve the inventory problem for the library.

As a recent development involving copyright problems similar to those of photocopying, I might mention that book publishers are beginning to bring out books which contain collections of reprints in given fields. For example, a book may include a number of reprints on "lasers" or some other rapidly developing field. If these reprints are from our journals, and many of them are, we attempt to collect from the publisher a royalty on the fraction of the articles which are taken from our journals equal to a similar fraction of 5 percent of the list price of the book. Also, we have been asked to permit the production and sale of microfilmed copies of volumes of our journals. In cases where we have copyrights, we have received a 10 percent royalty from the publisher of the microfilm copies.

If stamps were to be used to cover our losses, it would be my estimate that to break even the stamps should provide roughly 2 cents a page. Since an ordinary reprint averages about 8 to 10 pages, I would say, in order to offset our losses, we should be paid something of the order of 15 to 25 cents per photocopy.

Finally, I might add that while our objective, as stated in our charter, is to advance and diffuse knowledge of physics, we can only continue to do this if our income balances our expenses. Thus, while we invariably give permission to reprint from our journals on a single copy basis for scholarly purposes, we never give a blanket permission to reprint from our journals for commercial purposes without royalty. To do otherwise would mean that we would not be able to continue to perform the services for which we were established.

## John Markus

For several years a number of volunteer committees have been seeking an equitable solution to the problem of illegal photocopying of material from copyrighted books and magazines. Publishers consider the new photocopying machines to be a very real and immediate threat to essential communication among scientists and engineers through the medium of the printed word.

Many highly specialized scientific and engineering books—the types that are most highly valued by scientists and engineers—depend upon orders from specialized libraries for basic support. If unrestricted photocopying were to reduce the market for these books even a small amount, it would no longer be economically possible to publish them. This is why unrestricted photocopying will eventually impair rather than aid communication among scientists and engineers.

Photocopying of a copyrighted work in appreciable quantities is unquestionably illegal under our copyright laws. Furthermore, it is admitted that our courts have not as yet ruled on the doctrine of fair use, wherein a single copy is currently being made by many libraries and business firms for personal nonprofit use. On the other hand, some of our largest business firms, on advice of their legal counsel, prohibit their employees from making even single copies of copyrighted material without first obtaining permission from the copyright owner.

The music industry has solved its problem of encouraging the use of copyrighted material by setting up two clearing houses, ASCAP and BMI. Despite rather violent initial opposition, their systems are now working soundly and economically. Although the problems of the book and magazine publishing industry are somewhat different, and in some ways even more formidable, our committee feels that there is real hope for setting up a comparable copyright clearing house that will eventually be equally acceptable to publishers, authors, library copying services, and those who need photocopies. This report outlines the requirements of such a clearing house and presents one solution that shows promise of being economically feasible.

Any national or international copyright clearing house or other system for collecting royalties on photocopies of copyrighted material must meet the following nine requirements:

1. Satisfy the *copyright owners*. This means that a clearing house must provide for any reasonable combination of rates requested by publishers, including higher rates for certain types of material and prohibition of copying of certain items if requested. It also means that the cost of collecting and allocating the royalties must not exceed a reasonable percentage of the total royalties collected. Without the approval

of the publishers and/or authors who are the copyright owners, a clearing house cannot legally authorize photocopying of copyrighted works.

2. Require *minimum extra work* on the part of attendants in locations where copies are made, for collecting royalties and for collecting on a complete or sampling basis the data needed for allocating these royalties. Without the cooperation of these attendants, there is danger that illegal photocopying will continue.

3. Provide a rate schedule and system procedure that will appear *fair and reasonable to users* of photocopies, so as to obtain their cooperation and at the same time encourage increased dissemination of information through selective photocopying.

4. Be compatible with all *government regulations,* including copyright and anti-trust laws.

5. Be *legally enforceable.* This means that it must be possible to obtain legal evidence against deliberate infringers, to permit the filing of lawsuits against selected infringers so as to establish and publicize the legal authority of a copyright clearing house.

6. Be *operable on a partial basis,* since some copyright owners and some copying services may initially refuse to sign up.

7. Provide a simple means for *indicating on each photocopy* a notice indicating that it has been made legally and the appropriate royalty has been paid.

8. Provide a simple means for determining a fair *allocation of royalties* among publishers.

9. Provide for each publisher the data needed for allocating a share of these royalties among authors when and if such royalties reach an appreciable amount for an individual author.

## SPECIFICATIONS FOR A PHOTOCOPY ROYALTY SYSTEM

To establish a copyright clearing house that will meet the above nine major requirements and still be economical and practical, it appears highly desirable to meet some or all of the following additional system specifications:

1. There can be no free and uncontrolled copying of single copies of copyrighted material. This is an absolute specifica-

tion, because without it practically all of the photocopying being done today would continue to be done under a broad interpretation of the single-copy rule.

2. Publishers must receive an appreciable percentage of royalty income right from the beginning if they are to be expected to sign contracts that will turn over to a clearing house their legal right to enforce their copyright protection.

3. Setup costs of a clearing house must be amortized over a reasonable number of years if the preceding specification is to be met. This in turn means that a source of capital, preferably at low interest, must be located before a copyright clearing house can be established. A setup subsidy by some generous foundation would, of course, eliminate amortization.

4. The cost of establishing and operating a copyright clearing house, including the cost of collecting and allocating royalties, should be under 50 percent of the total royalties collected. The exact initial percentage will depend on the royalty rates established for each page copied and on the number of years chosen for amortization of setup costs.

5. A copyright clearing house must operate initially on the honor system, because the cost of establishing and operating an even partly cheatproof system would be prohibitively high. The honor system is considered to be practical because most librarians are inherently honest and most business firms will not deliberately ignore a law *if given a reasonable way to obey it.*

6. Provision must be made for collecting royalties on a bulk or license-fee basis from industrial and business firms who want to do their photocopying legally but would rebel at preparing accurate unit records.

7. The system must include a royalty rate book, with supplements or new editions as required. These books must be carefully planned for ease of use, and must tell when there is no need to pay a royalty.

8. The system must be operable initially without requiring publishers to print special notices, codes, or other data in their works.

9. The system must be applicable to all types of copying or duplicating machines, present or future, including microimage, magnetic tape, and other media for disseminating copy-

righted material. This means that techniques involving modifications of copying machines are not likely to be practical.

## DESCRIPTION OF PROPOSED PHOTOCOPY ROYALTY SYSTEM

The basic framework of one possible royalty collecting and distributing system that meets the preceding requirements and specifications will now be described. This presentation will include many clearly stated estimates and assumptions, each of which must be verified or corrected during subsequent detailed studies. It is felt that the use of numerical examples, even though based on guesses, will help to evaluate the merits of the proposed system and will stimulate proposals for even more economical and practical systems.

The main features of the proposed copyright clearing house system will be described in the following order:

1. Photocopy order slips
2. Imprinter-counter for photocopies
3. Rate book
4. Report forms
5. Sorting procedure for slips
6. Accounting procedure
7. Allocating royalties to authors
8. Self-service installations

1. *Photocopy Order Slips.* At the majority of copying services in libraries and elsewhere, a request for photocopies is usually made in writing on a printed form, much as when requesting a book at a library. For magazines, this form generally calls for the name of the magazine, the issue date, and the page numbers to be copied. These forms may also contain spaces for filling in the amount to be charged the user for making the photocopies. Such copying charges range from 10 to 45 cents per page, generally with a minimum charge, and sometimes also with a handling charge, a service charge, and other fixed charges per order.

It is conceivable that a standard photocopy order slip could be designed that would meet the requirements of all copying services for their own ordering and accounting purposes and at the same time provide input data for a clearing house. If copying services need these slips for their own records, a two-part carbon-interleaved form could be used instead.

One important advantage of the proposed slip system is the fact that the person desiring the copy does most of the work of filling out the slip. The copying service merely collects the slips and ships them to the clearing house in envelopes or boxes provided for this purpose.

The slip system should meet the requirements of information centers that distribute copies of articles, because such a center will have to fill out some types of slip to order the desired copying. An operational clearing house thus paves the way for fully legal operation of information centers on a commercial basis for profit.

The slip system applies equally well to internal information centers that distribute copies of articles selectively or on demand to their own employees. Here only the total number of copies made of each article needs to be recorded.

The data on the photocopy order slips would provide invaluable raw material for use by researchers in analyzing the nature and extent of photocopying on a nationwide basis. It is possible that financial support for sorting the slips and carrying out analyical research could be obtained either by the nonprofit clearing house or by individual researchers or universities to whom the slips were made available.

Tabulations of magazine pages copied would be useful to publishers as *reader feedback* on a nationwide scale, since page numbers are clues to the articles that readers consider worthy of wider dissemination. Such feedback could guide publishers in planning editorial balance for future magazine issues. Similar data on book pages copied could also be of use in planning book publishing programs.

The handwritten slips can be sorted at the clearing house at any time during the following accounting period, by book publisher and by magazine, using low-salaried part-time or full-time clerical help. The slips could then be shipped to the publishers, for such analyses as they care to make and for allocation of authors' shares of royalties.

2. *Imprinter-Counter for Photocopies.* Each photocopy for which a fee is collected should carry some indication that the copy had been made legally and the fee paid. A simple manually operated printing, embossing, or punching device can be used, perhaps like a notary public's seal. The device could have a built-in counter that advances each time the operating lever of the

imprinter is actuated, to indicate the total number of copies that had been imprinted during an accounting period.

The imprint in the margin of a photocopy should show the name insignia of the clearing house and wording indicating that a royalty had been paid. This will make the purchaser of the copy feel that he is getting something tangible for the extra fee that he pays.

If several different rates are to be charged, and the rates are multiples of a unit rate, the imprint can be applied the appropriate number of times in the margin of the photocopy to correspond to the rate for that copy. (The alternative of a rate-printing device like a Pitney-Bowes postage meter would be more difficult to use and prohibitively costly.)

If some equivalent of a Bates numbering machine is used as the imprinter, it would place on the photocopy an ink-stamped serial number comparable to a counter reading, eliminating the need for a separate counter. The number imprinted on the last copy made during an accounting period is then used with the number recorded for the previous period, to obtain by subtraction the total copies.

Embossing is an attractive alternate possibility for placing an imprint on each photocopy. For embossing, a counter can be attached to a variation of a notary public seal. The embossed designation has the psychological merit of looking impressive and legal, and requires no replenishing of ink. An embossing device sold at $3.75 for use on letterheads may be applicable; this retail price includes three lines of up to 21 characters each, which could be:

COPYING ROYALTY PAID

TO COPYRIGHT

CLEARING HOUSE

3. *Rate Book.* Clear and simple instructions will be needed for determining whether a royalty should be collected on a given photocopy and determining the correct rate. This could be a frequently updated instruction booklet listing the publishers who have signed copying contracts, giving rates, and indicating which publications, if any, can be photocopied free. Any restrictions on copying, as of special charts or maps, would also have to be listed. The simpler the rate and contract structures, the less will be the cost of this booklet.

Many cross-reference entries will be needed in the rate book, because names of publishers and magazines change frequently.

This book will have to be planned with extreme care to make it easy to use; if not, impatient users may ignore the system and gamble that they won't get caught.

Copying services should place on their customers the responsibility for showing that the desired material is available for free copying or that it can be copied for a particular rate per page. This means that the user will have to refer to the rate book. This seems reasonable, because it is the user who benefits most from photocopying. If the copying service attendant were required to look up the rate and there was a requirement for collecting a royalty each time copies were made, there would undoubtedly be objections from the copying services.

Some magazines run fractional columns of editorial turnover and editorial pages at the back of an issue. The rate book should cover this. One possibility is to collect a royalty on every page copied, even if a part of the page is advertising. Any other procedure would involve a rather complex estimating process that would be confusing to users and copying service attendants. The minimum royalty on an article would be that for one full page, even though the article is a short item occupying less than a page.

4. *Report Forms*. In addition to supplying the photocopy order forms, a clearing house would have to provide simple report forms and self-addressed envelopes or shipping boxes. The envelopes or boxes would be used for storing and eventually shipping the accumulated photocopy order slips, the royalty checks, and the royalty-totalizing report forms. It may also be desirable to provide accounting report forms for checking daily royalty receipts against the reading of the counter on the imprinter.

The report form could be a pad of sheets, each having 31 lines so as to serve for one month. To encourage use of the form, it can provide colums for data needed for photocopy cost accounting as well.

The photocopy order slips coming to the clearing house can immediately be dumped into one big hopper. The only function of these slips here is to determine the fair allocation of royalties received, even though some are based only on counter readings and have no publisher data. It is expected that the sample will be somewhere between 50 and 60 percent of the total copies made, in contrast to ASCAP where the allocation is based on a sample of only about 1 percent of total music played. Treating the slips as sampling data eliminates the costly normal rechecking of subtotals and totals after each sort.

5. *Sorting Procedure for Slips.* The photocopy order slips coming to the clearing house at the end of each accounting period will have to be sorted manually by publisher and/or magazine. This type of sort will cost around 1 cent per slip.

The handwritten slips can be designed for conversion with minimum key-punching effort to punched tape or IBM punched cards, for use as data input to a computer that would compute the percentages for allocation of surplus income to publishers. Since a given slip represents an average of five copies, the cost of key-punching would be spread over royalties from these five copies. It remains to be shown, however, whether computer processing will save any money over conventional manual processing for the simple sorting, adding, and other elementary bookkeeping operations involved in the proposed system.

6. *Accounting Procedure.* After sorting of slips, the totalizing of royalties per publisher would probably be most economical as a simple, old-fashioned adding-machine operation. Since a clearing house will undoubtedly have to face annual auditing of its records, the adding-machine tapes would have to be labeled and saved. The slips could be microfilmed inexpensively on automatic microfilm cameras (about 1/10 cent per slip), so microfilm copies would be available for auditing and for research studies after the slips were shipped to the publishers.

The total royalties recorded on slips for each publisher are added together to obtain a grand total. The ratio of total recorded royalty for a publisher to the grand total of recorded royalties is now computed, to give the percentage to be used in allocating net income for that accounting period, after deduction of expenses.

7. *Allocating Royalties to Authors.* The allocation of copying royalty income by a publisher to his authors can be done with no additional effort or expense if the proposed slip system is used and the format of the slip is properly planned initially. For books, only identification of the book by title and edition is needed, along with the number of pages copied and the number of copies made of each page. Names of authors do not have to be entered, because the publisher will have to use his own royalty schedules for apportioning royalties among coauthors (coauthor royalties are often related to the portion of the book done by each, hence may not be equal shares).

It is unlikely that any magazines will make a distribution to authors of individual articles. Instead, the magazines could use copying royalty income to increase their page rate of payment to future authors or reduce the amount of per-page subsidy requested from the author's organization. It should be noted that any magazine can make an allocation to its authors if desired, however. The page numbers reported on a copy-ordering slip serve to identify the authors who are being copied. A magazine publisher can thus make such an allocation to any or all of his authors whenever he desires, merely by sorting his batch of slips by title, then totalizing copying royalties by title and determining percentages for author allocations.

8. *Self-Service Installations.* For self-service installations, such as those of Xerox 914 machines used for internal copying needs in industry and business, there can be no on-the-spot collection of royalties and probably no photocopy order slips. Here an imprinter-counter and a rate book would be provided for each machine, to meet the desire of these groups to pay royalties where appropriate. Some person in each company would then have to read the counters at the end of each accounting period and send in the report forms.

It is estimated that there are now close to 5,000 unattended coin-in-the-slot wet-process copying machines in use. These can take books and magazines, and are often in libraries, hence must also be considered by a clearing house. Here there are real problems for a clearing house unless arrangements can be made to include an average royalty fee with the amount inserted in each machine to pay for the photocopy.

## ESTIMATED INCOME OF CLEARING HOUSE

1. *Number of Copying Services.* Today most of the copying of copyrighted material is being done from bound books and magazines. The Xerox 914 Copier dominates this field, with an estimated 40,000 machines now in use.

The number of other makes of book copiers in use is small by comparison (probably around 5,000). There are probably also a few hundred Photostat machines still being used in libraries for photocopying. Some copying is being done from microfilm on reader-printers, but the amount here is also small.

The duplication of complete books and magazines from microfilm on large Xerox Copyflo machines is largely being done legally today, under contract with or by permission of the copyright owners.

Although we may have a potential of over 45,000 machines

today that are capable of copying books and magazines, only a fraction of these are actually being used for this purpose. (The others are being used chiefly for correspondence and business forms.)

One guidepost to copying services that are today selling copies of copyrighted material is *Directory of Library Photoduplication Services*, published in February 1962 by the University of Chicago Library. This lists 371 libraries in the U. S. having some kind of photocopy service (plus 12 more in Canada and Mexico). This figure is based on only 390 replies to a mailing of 2,848 questionnaires, and cannot therefore be considered a complete report. Furthermore, of the 20,000-odd Xerox 914 installations made since the questionnaire was mailed in 1961, many undoubtedly went into libraries. For these reasons, we are assuming that if a clearing house is established in the near future there will be about 1,000 copying services *that charge for copies* and can be signed up as members.

In many organizations, books and magazines are copied on a self-service basis on Xerox 914 machines, with no payments and hence no records. In addition, there are reported to be close to 5,000 coin-in-the-slot Documat and Federal Vico-Matic book copiers in the U. S. today. (These are wet-process machines giving a white-on-black negative copy, usually for 25 cents.) We must assume that users of these machines will want to pay royalties on photocopies also. This can be done by providing for each machine a rate book, appropriate instructions, and an imprinter-counter, together with special report forms. Many details remain to be worked out for these installations. For the present, let us assume that there will be a total of 10,000 such self-service installations that would pay royalties on the basis of imprinter-counter readings only.

2. *Number of Book Publishers.* In 1962, according to *Publishers' Weekly*, there were 470 active book publishers in the U. S. (active being defined as producing more than five titles in the year), plus 12 "cooperative" or "vanity" publishers. Many other publishers produced one to five books each per year, but their number is not known. Until more accurate figures can be obtained, then it would seem logical to assume a figure of 500 book publishers as a basis for estimating sorting and royalty-allocating costs.

3. *Number of Magazine Publishers.* In 1962, *Ayer's Directory* listed 9,643 magazines being published in the U. S., excluding

house organs, school magazines, and others having chiefly internal circulation. According to one estimate, only about 60 percent of these are copyrighted. This means that slips will have to be sorted and surplus royalties allocated to a maximum of about 6,000 magazines.

4. *Number of Copies.* If the foregoing statistical estimates are reasonably correct, we can make the assumption that our copyright clearing house will receive batches of slips from about 1,000 copying services at the end of each accounting period for sorting into a maximum of 6,500 piles.

Let us assume, in lieu of actual survey figures, that the average monthly output of each library copying service is 5,000 copies of all types. If we further assume that half of the material is copyrighted, we have 2,500 copies per month from our 1,000 copying services, or 30,000 copies per year, on which royalties are to be collected.

The average copy order is generally assumed as being five pages. Dividing the 30,000 copies per year by five gives an average of 6,000 slips per year per copying service (slightly less than 25 slips per day), or 6,000,000 each year for sorting.

We previously assumed that an additional 10,000 self-service machines would pay royalties based on imprinter-counter use. If an average library copying service pays royalty on 30,000 copies per year, it seems logical to assume that a machine in business or industry would give only around 2,000 royalty counts per year. Multiplying 2,000 by 10,000 such self-service installations gives 20,000,000 more copies (more strictly, unit royalties) producing clearing-house income.

5. *Estimated Income.* What will total *annual royalty income* be? The base for making this estimate is 30,000,000 copies per year on which royalties are collected by means of photocopy order slips, plus 20,000,000 self-service copies on which royalties are collected from counter readings, or a total of 50,000,000 royalty-paid copies per year. Assuming a single average per-page royalty rate for the time being, gross annual income can be figured for various royalty rates as follows:

| Avg. Page Rate, Cents | Income from Copying Services | Income from Self-Service Machines | Total Income |
|---|---|---|---|
| 1 | $1,000 \times 30,000 \times .01 = \$ 300,000$ | $10,000 \times 2,000 \times .01 = \$ 200,000$ | $ 500,000 |
| 2 | $1,000 \times 30,000 \times .02 = 600,000$ | $10,000 \times 2,000 \times .02 = 400,000$ | 1,000,000 |
| 3 | $1,000 \times 30,000 \times .03 = 900,000$ | $10,000 \times 2,000 \times .03 = 600,000$ | 1,500,000 |
| 4 | $1,000 \times 30,000 \times .04 = 1,200,000$ | $10,000 \times 2,000 \times .04 = 800,000$ | 2,000,000 |
| 5 | $1,000 \times 30,000 \times .05 = 1,500,000$ | $10,000 \times 2,000 \times .05 = 1,000,000$ | 2,500,000 |

It cannot be emphasized too much that the foregoing estimates are *guesses* at this time, with very few facts on which to base them. They are presented here in lieu of anything better now, to give a report format in which more accurate figures can be substituted from time to time as they become available.

## ESTIMATED EXPENSES

Expenses fall into two categories:

1. *Setup Expenses.* These expenses, estimated at $1,000,000, will be incurred over a period of one to two years before royalties start coming in at the end of the first accounting period. Such one-time expenses should presumably be amortized over a number of years. If there are no setup subsidies, total setup expenses and interest on this amount over the amortization period can be divided by estimated pages copied under royalty during this period, to get a cost-per-page amortization figure to be considered when establishing rates.

A reasonable period for amortizing setup costs might be five years. With no subsidy, this money would have to be borrowed during the two-year setup period and paid back over the first five-year period of royalty income. The interest rate on a loan from a foundation might be as low as 2 percent, but a commercial rate of 5 percent will be assumed here to be conservative. This interest would be paid on the declining balance, so let us say that it corresponds to full interest for three years. Thus, $3 \times 5\% \times$ $1,000,000 is $150,000 total interest. This gives total setup costs of $1,150,000 to be amortized in five years by income from an estimated $5 \times 50,000,000$ copies $= 250,000,000$ copies (the income growth rate being unknown, a constant royalty income from 50 million pages per year is assumed here). Dividing $1,150,000 by 250,000,000 gives 46/100 cent per page, or roughly ½ cent per page for five years to amortize the setup cost.

2. *Operating Expenses.* These are the annual expenses incurred during actual operation, such as office rental, executive staff salaries, continuing publicity expense, contract procurement, and renewal costs, additional imprinter-counters and supplies needed for new and old affiliates, and all clerical expenses associated with processing of slips and royalties. The total for one year is estimated at $537,000.

With an assumed 50,000,000 pages per year producing royalties, we divide $537,000 by 50,000,000 and get slightly over 1 cent as the operating cost per page (per unit royalty) after the clearing house has been set up. If there is no subsidy for setup, adding ½ cent setup cost to the 1 cent operating cost gives 1½ cents per page as total clearing house cost per copy on which royalty is collected. If our initial goal is distribution of about half of the income to publishers, we arrive at 3 cents per page as a likely unit royalty rate, based on the *assumed* parameters of this report.

Once setup costs have been written off, operating experience is gained, more copying services are signed up, and copying costs come down to a point where still more copying is being done, the expenses of a copyright clearing house per unit of royalty collected will inevitably drop. This can mean both a lower unit royalty rate and a greater return to publishers, so as to encourage publication of still more books.

### William N. Locke

I have two comments.* One is that your statement refers to the library whose collections are available to the public without charge. Many private colleges including mine do not have the library available without charge. We cannot possibly afford to. We are in a big city; we are already swamped. This wording, then, is very unfair to M.I.T. and, I am sure, to Harvard and a great many other urban private colleges. You should try to cover us.

On the other hand, don't bother because I shan't be embarrassed. On advice of counsel, I shall refuse to pay royalties. Moreover, so will all the members of the ARL, SLA, ALA, and all the other library organizations who have what we think is sound advice of counsel to the effect that we can make one copy of any copyrighted work for anybody.

I am not concerned by your royalty cost, but I am concerned about your statement that about 50 percent of the material that is copied now is copyrighted; the other 50 percent is not. I am wondering how the operator of this photocopying machine is going to distinguish quickly whether he is to charge or not. I see a decision process that is going to cost us more than the actual cost of copying.

### John Markus

You have hit on another real problem. The rate book is our

*Editor's note:* The first comment refers to a point made by a previous speaker which was omitted from this published version. However, the response remains an interesting one and is retained.

answer, but it is not going to be simple if the publishers are going to insist on varying rates, as I am afraid they will.

## Samuel Freedman

I understood Mr. Kuney to have said that in my talk I said that microfiche is available at no cost. This is not the case, as far as I recall. The point I wished to make is that cost estimates that I provided (Chapter 2) did not include royalties to publishers. It has been our policy and will continue to be our policy as an ethical copier to pay royalties to whatever publisher will permit us to copy his material. Actually, we don't have such permission from all the publishers, which is a difficult situation for us competitively.

## Joseph Kuney

Figures that are always given as the cost of information retrieval never include, in the big bracket figure, the cost that goes into preparation; this is always a footnote.

## Samuel Freedman

I sympathize with your points of view, but it won't be possible to include those figures in any total because there is no way to determine in advance what that figure will be.

## William N. Locke

These can be estimated on the basis of royalty figures at a couple of cents a page, which we have just been given. I don't see why you can't put this estimate in.

## Allen Kent

There was one point that was not brought out in this copyright discussion that I think might go on record. This relates to the fact that we are talking about a National Science Library System—and the emphasis is on *Science*. The statement has been made by Dr. Hutchisson and perhaps by Joseph Kuney that publication is a necessary part of research work. Now, if we consider that most scientific endeavors going on in our country are supported by government, then why not use the same principle that is used often in connection with patents resulting from government-supported work? That is, the government is permitted royalty-free use of the material for whatever purposes it deems necessary.

John Markus

I believe the government should include photocopy royalties as part of its contract awards to those who need photocopies.

Joseph Kuney

That is the point I was trying to make. It doesn't make any difference what you call it. The fact remains that the cost for preparing information for the primary publication has somehow got to be paid. If the totality of the situation is such that the copying problem will not hinder this aim, then it is kind of self-solving. But it is not solved if the amount of copying does affect the income of the publisher to the point where he is unable to publish. Somehow the bill has to be paid, and that is the only point I am trying to make. I am not talking about the rightness or the wrongness. I am trying to illustrate that this is the problem. It is not one of "Are we copying legally or illegally?" We are all concerned with the problem of maintaining the flow of information. We are starting it; you are pushing it along the way. But how do we keep it going?

Allen Kent
(as Chairman)

I think that is really a good, positive point on which to end the conference. We have had some very simple objectives in connection with this conference. First, was to examine the National Science Library System report which is still in draft form. Second, we were to examine the first step that might be taken to implement the program, that is, to establish control of source materials using microform. Third, to obtain opinions regarding copyright implications of the plan. I would say that the job is done to the very great satisfaction of Dr. Warren. He has obtained the opinions he sought. He promised that they will be taken into account, and suggested further that there will be another chance, upon reflection, to comment on this proposed program when hearings are held in Washington.

# Index

# Index